THE ACTORS' DIRECTOR

For Christine, Iain and Stuart and to the memory of my parents

The ACTORS' DIRECTOR

RICHARD ATTENBOROUGH BEHIND THE CAMERA

Introduction by Steven Spielberg

ANDY DOUGAN

MAINSTREAM
PUBLISHING

EDINBURGH AND LONDON

The publisher gratefully acknowledges George McKechnie and the *Evening Times* for permission to reproduce the photograph on page 6, and Phil Caruso for the photograph of Richard Attenborough on the set of *Miracle on 34th Street*.

First published in Great Britain in 1994 by
MAINSTREAM PUBLISHING COMPANY (EDINBURGH) LTD
7 Albany Street
Edinburgh EH1 3UG

ISBN 1 85158 672 5

A catalogue record for this book is available from the British Library

Typeset in Janson and Optima by Litho Link Ltd,
Powys, Wales

Printed in Great Britain by Butler and Tanner Ltd, Frome

Contents

Acknowledgments and Author's Note

For what is supposed to be a solitary endeavour, writing this book would not have been possible without the help and support of a great many people.

One of the aims of this book is to show that, as the screenwriter William Goldman once said, 'directing is hard work – like coalmining is hard work'. To that end, Richard Attenborough's thoughts are presented here as they were articulated in a series of taped interviews. With the exception of removing my questions, I have tried as much as possible to preserve his answers as he gave them.

It goes without saying that I am deeply indebted to Richard Attenborough for his patience and co-operation and also for making available the resources of his extensive photographic archive. But perhaps more than that I am grateful to Diana Hawkins for her tireless efforts on my behalf as well as her constructive suggestions. No one knows Richard Attenborough the film-maker better and she should be the one writing this book. I am deeply grateful that she has never found the time.

My thanks also go to everyone who agreed to be interviewed for the book to provide their perspective on working with Richard Attenborough. I am grateful to them all, but especially to Steven Spielberg, William Goldman and Sir John Mills for the way in which they allowed me to inconvenience them. I am also grateful to all those who helped set up the interviews. Special thanks go to Stephanie Wenborn and Clare Thornton for their efforts during the *Shadowlands* tour and to Ken Green and everyone else at United International Pictures who contributed greatly to smoothing my path.

To Quentin Falk my thanks for help in avoiding the traps for young players, and to Siobhan Synnot my gratitude for access to the material she gathered during her interview with Richard Attenborough.

My thanks also to everyone at Mainstream, especially my very patient editor, Peter Frances. I am also grateful to Peter Dunne, Gabriel Clare-Hunt and everyone at Beaver Lodge, Alison Webb, Judy Wasdell, Jane Garner, Gerry Lewis, Andrew Dann, Wendy Kidd, George McKechnie, Russell Kyle and especially Peter Scott.

Preface

Over the course of a career which spans more than 50 years, Richard Attenborough has become synonymous with the British film industry. After graduating from RADA Attenborough starred on the London stage in plays such as *Brighton Rock* and *The Little Foxes*. He also achieved notable stage success with his wife, Sheila Sim, in, first, *To Dorothy A Son* and, most notably, in the very first London production of *The Mousetrap*. Before graduating from RADA the young Attenborough had already made his screen debut in *In Which We Serve* after being spotted in a London repertory company. This 1942 movie was produced, written and directed by Noel Coward with the intention of boosting wartime morale. It was also the directing début of David Lean and there is a certain symmetry in two of the great international names of the British cinema starting their film careers on the same picture.

While training as a pilot Attenborough was seconded to the Royal Air Force Film Unit and in 1944 made *Journey Together*. The film was directed by John Boulting and had Edward G. Robinson as a guest star. The Hollywood star helped shape Attenborough's acting style and the British director was a seminal influence on the way Attenborough himself would work with actors.

It was Boulting who gave Attenborough his first distinctive screen role, re-creating the psychotic Pinky in the screen version of *Brighton Rock*. From there many more memorable performances followed in acclaimed films such as *Morning Departure, Dunkirk, The Angry Silence, The League of Gentlemen, The Great Escape, Séance on a Wet Afternoon, Guns at Batasi, The Sand Pebbles, Dr Dolittle* and, possibly his finest screen performance, *10 Rillington Place*, in which he played mass-murderer John Reginald Christie.

By the late Fifties Attenborough had already moved into producing. He and his partner, fellow actor turned screenwriter Bryan Forbes, had become disillusioned and disenchanted with the state of the British film industry.

Together they formed Beaver Films, which was responsible for landmark British films such as *The Angry Silence, Séance on a Wet Afternoon* and *Whistle Down the Wind.*

It was more than 25 years after starting his career as an actor that Attenborough stepped behind the camera to direct for the first time. The film was *Oh! What A Lovely War*, although Attenborough had long intended his début would be made with his long-cherished dream of a film of the life of Mahatma Gandhi.

Since that start in 1969 Attenborough has made nine films as a director. Each has added to his reputation as one of the major names in world cinema. None more so than *Gandhi*, which he finally brought to the screen, earning eight Oscars in the process, including two for himself, for Best Director and Best Film. No other British film has won more Oscars, and *Gandhi* also won five BAFTA awards in the same year. Each of his films is typified by his own unique blend of courage and sentiment. Whether it is on a massive endeavour such as *A Bridge Too Far* or a more intimate venture such as *Shadowlands* he is an uncompromising director. He has been praised to the heavens and condemned to the depths. He has taken stands of commendable courage against the biggest studios in the business and defended his position to the last. He fights like a tiger for his choices and his actors love him for it.

His efforts on behalf of the British film industry earned him a knighthood in 1976. Last year he was elevated to the peerage and may now be formally addressed as The Rt. Hon The Lord Attenborough of Richmond-upon-Thames.

But first and foremost Attenborough is a consummate film-maker, admired and respected by great names among his peers such as Steven Spielberg. He is a man who is never happier than on the studio floor with his actors. And he is a man who is, above all else, an actors' director.

Introduction

had met Dickie Attenborough at various functions over the years, but I don't
think I ever felt so much fondness on a personal basis for Dickie as I did when
we were both in competition for the 1982 Directors Guild of America
Award. He was nominated for *Gandhi*, and I was nominated for *ET.* Dickie won,
but he went out of his way to embrace me before going up on to the podium
to collect the award. That meant a great deal to me then, as it does now.

Before 1982, however, I had another very unique experience involving
Dickie. I was flirting with making a movie from the William Goldman book,
Magic. I had talked to Robert De Niro about playing the part that Anthony
Hopkins wound up playing, and I really wanted to direct the movie. At the
time, it didn't go to me; it went to Dickie Attenborough. I had it in my mind
how I would have made that film, and I thought it would have been pretty good.
After a year had gone by, and Dickie's film opened in theatres, I went to see the
picture and realized that it was a hell of a lot better than what I would have
done.

Although I can't speak about how Dickie is valued in Britain, I know that
in the United States he is a prize. Producers feel lucky if Dickie says 'yes' to an
American project. Dickie will often say 'no', because as a film-maker he likes
to engender his own projects. He likes to plant his own seeds and place the
bulbs himself, one of his most endearing qualities. I think that's why when
people discuss Dickie Attenborough, they discuss him not as a 'movie director',
they talk about him as a 'film-maker'. To me, there is a big distinction between
the two. A 'movie director' is someone who is a director for hire, and a 'film-
maker' is someone who isn't really for hire and makes his or her own pictures
in a style that is unmistakably personal and unique.

I know that Dickie and I are of different movie-making generations
chronologically, but it doesn't make any difference. There is no such thing as

'generations' among movie directors or film-makers, because we drink from the same source. Our well-springs are Kurosawa, David Lean, Antonioni, Fellini, Truffaut, Ford, Hawks, Capra, Hitchcock, and many, many others. We all steal from the same people, providing of course they are the best people.

Like many of these 'well-springs', Dickie is famous for his persistence and his perseverance. These are qualities that don't actually make it up on to the screen, but they are the reason each film became possible in the first place. Over the years, Dickie has made a lot of impossible concepts into very commercial and fully realized stories. And I think one of the things that distinguishes him from other film-makers is that he loves biographies. He is a contemporary, classical film biographer. He is also a quintessential actor's director. Dickie is a good director because he leaves the actor to play the melody while he does all the harmonizing.

Dickie is also a director's director. I remember at one stage when I was simultaneously involved in the shooting of *Schindler's List* and the post-production of *Jurassic Park*, I asked Dickie if he would take over the filming of *Schindler's List* for a few days. He was busy with *Shadowlands* at the time, so he wasn't able to do it. But I asked him because, of all my colleagues, he is the only person who I think really understood what I was trying to do with *Schindler's List*.

And in the final analysis, the simple fact that I would trust him with several days on *Schindler's List* is the best way I know of telling you what I think of Dickie Attenborough.

Steven Spielberg
May, 1994

Oh! What A Lovely Start

I was given the script for *Oh! What A Lovely War* by Sir John Mills. I had worked with John lots of times as an actor in films such as *Dunkirk*, *Morning Departure* and *In Which We Serve* which was, of course, my own first film. He is something of a hero of mine, as I think he should be to a lot of actors because he is genuinely one of the unsung heroes of the British film industry. If you go back over the catalogue of his movies they make a staggering list. He is caricatured as a stiff-upper-lip member of the upper-deck type and is also, I think, slightly dismissed by virtue of the fact that people say, 'Oh, he's only a film actor'. The great thing about John Mills is that he, and perhaps James Mason, was to change the whole attitude of the profession towards acting in the cinema. He made cinema performing respectable. You were no longer seen as just being there for the money, there really was something to create. Prior to the war all of our cinema emanated from the theatre and was performed like theatre. John Mills understood what acting in the cinema could be. He established himself in the same league and bracket as the Americans before we started doing our own pictures during the war and developing a style of our own. So professionally that's one of the reasons why he is a great hero of mine.

I had been trying to make a film about Mahatma Gandhi since 1962 and when I decided I wanted to do it naturally John Mills was one of the very first people I talked to. He knew, not that I wanted to direct, but that I wanted specifically to direct *Gandhi*. I'd ring him up from time to time and cry on his shoulder. 'I'm skint Johnny,' I'd say, 'I don't know what to do, I don't know where to go.' We went through all of that stuff and the upshot was that he knew that I was interested and intrigued by directing even though it was for a particular instance. I came home one day and there was a script at home and a note from Johnny. We both lived in Richmond at the time, we were on

13

the Green and he and Mary lived up the hill. He said he would love me to read it, he would be up until about 11 and I should ring him after I'd read it. The script was for Joan Littlewood's musical *Oh! What A Lovely War*. I read it and I rang around 11 and said, 'Boy what a fabulous subject, I wouldn't have thought it would have moved so successfully to the screen, it's wonderfully atmospheric. There's lots of potential there for lots of ideas. But I'm a little puzzled,' I told him. 'I don't know what you want me to play? What are you suggesting?'

And he said, 'I'm not suggesting that you should play anything; I'm suggesting that you should direct'.

I said, 'You must be bloody mad, I can't direct this, I wouldn't know what to do.' I said, 'Why Johnny? How?'

He told me that he and Len Deighton, who had written the script, had decided they could go one of two ways. Either they could go for someone who knew everything and had vast experience and was armed with ideas of how it might be done, and in the process take the risk that they might perhaps be doing things that had been done before. Or they could go to somebody who knew absolutely bugger all and would perhaps open some new doors and introduce some fresh ideas. 'We decided,' he told me, 'on the latter.' And that is genuinely how my directing début came about.

Looking back I think it was a kind of miracle because circumstances can vary so greatly in differing situations. I always remember Peter Brook's first major directing venture in London, with *Shadow and Substance* at the Ambassadors Theatre. It was a subject which permitted him to move out of the normal theatrical convention and it took the audience by surprise. Now I might have been asked to direct *Morning Departure* in 1949 and no matter how well I might have directed it, no matter how good the performances were, the actual shooting had to be conventional, even mundane. The wonderful thing from my point of view about *Oh! What A Lovely War* was the fact that you could do anything. Indeed you were likely to do things that nobody had ever done before, nobody had ever witnessed, and that nobody had ever conceived. So by doing that suddenly you are, in quotes, a director. It was probably that fact more than any other that got me going as a director – not my actual skill, or lack of it, but the opportunity, the unique opportunity which was there for me to grab.

There are a couple of scenes in the movie which people always talk about. They're the ones that they suggest no experienced director would touch – the shooting-gallery scene near the start and the final shot of all those crosses. The suggestion is usually that these are shots that I attempted because I didn't know they really ought not to have been done.

The shooting gallery scene was played by a lovely actor called Paul Shelley. He and the Smith family are on the pier for the day out and Paul was at a shooting gallery aiming at little targets. What I wanted to do was to move Paul, rather than merely cutting, from that circumstance to the trenches. We started to track all the way round away from Paul, up on to the target, on to the various figures that were on the shooting gallery, and we came back all

Attenborough rehearses a camera movement on *Oh! What A Lovely War*

the way round on to Paul again. By this time three prop men and two wardrobe people had totally stripped Paul of all his clothes, put on a new zip uniform, stuck a tin hat on him, replaced the rifle and put sandbags over the top of the area where the shooting gallery was now transformed into a salient. It was in a way cumbersome but in terms of emotion it took the audience absolutely with you without any break whatsoever. The easiest thing obviously would have been to dissolve or to cut or whatever the conventional solution was. And the surprise of saying, 'that's where he is in fantasy but this is where he is in reality' took the audience with it. It reinforced, I think, the fact that statements made on the pier were just as pertinent and just as important as the actual reality so I wanted desperately to do it in a single movement and happily we managed to pull it off.

The end shot was the very first scene I thought of. Everybody said it was completely out of the question. You have to remember that this was 1969, which is 25 years ago, and there were no computers and the possibility of hi-tech special effects like digital matte shots simply didn't exist if that is indeed what you wanted to do. But I didn't want to do that. I wanted to start on that one boy's grave, that one cross, and then pull back. The audience should be saying to itself subconsciously, 'there can't be more, there cannot be more, you cannot go further' to the point where they are almost out of breath. But of course there are more and in the end the screen is absolutely filled with these tiny white crosses.

In those days there was only one way to get a shot like that and that was by using a helicopter. And I can't remember how many Saturdays we rehearsed – six, eight, ten Saturdays – before we got a helicopter movement that would work. The one thing I always remember was that we had a marvellous art director called Don Ashton. He could best be epitomised by the fact that the rest of us could be out on a recce to find a suitable location to deputise for the Western Front or whatever it was. We would be in Wellington boots and filthy clothes and as we emerged from that sludge pit of muck, with us would come Don Ashton and you could still see your face in his shoes. He was the most immaculate man I have ever met. We discussed the end shot and I remember him saying, 'If that's what you want, that's what you shall have. That's what we must do for you.' No more was said and we went on to discuss other aspects of the production and all of this was forgotten. As far as everyone was concerned that was how it was going to be, it was going to be done by a helicopter and that would be it. I then remember

Attenborough and Ralph Richardson between takes on *Oh! What A Lovely War*

Vanessa Redgrave hangs on her director's every word on *Oh! What A Lovely War*

Don coming on to the set ashen-faced about three weeks after we'd gone into production. He said, 'Dick, I know it's the last shot of the picture, I know it means absolutely everything to you and I know I said you could have it, but I'm afraid it's out of the question. The whole of the Sussex Downs are chalk, you can't hammer the crosses in, you've got to drill a hole.' In total I think there were something like 15,000 crosses but I'm afraid I stood my ground and insisted that we did it the way I had planned. So the crosses were duly drilled in and we got the shot and it works very well.

Having agreed to direct the film, we were then faced with the perennial problem of raising the money to make it. One of the people we approached was Charles Bludhorn, the indomitable head of Paramount Pictures. These days Hollywood favours the 25-word pitch but in 1969 I did the whole movie of *Oh! What A Lovely War* for Bludhorn. Not every single line but I did all the numbers and the dances for him at the Dorchester. Because I can sing a bit, I could cope with all the songs and I also managed an assimilation of some of the dances and at the end of it he said, 'Who are you going to have in it?'

Apart from John Mills, of course, I hadn't even thought of that so, lying through my teeth, I said, 'Olivier, Richardson, Gielgud, Redgrave, Maggie Smith, Dirk Bogarde, Jack Hawkins, Kenneth More,' and reeled off almost every name I could think of.

His chin dropped further and further as the list went on. I stood my ground and insisted that was the sort of cast this picture had to have and he said to

me, 'You get me five – with Olivier – and you have the money.'

I came out of the Dorchester and I practically fainted. I mean I knew all of them but I knew also that Olivier was the key and if I could get him I could get the rest. Larry had always said to me the days of the actor–manager had been lost, the actor–manager must make a return so I knew the fact that I was going to produce and direct would be the kind of thing that he would want to hear. I went to Brighton and unfortunately he wasn't very well. I went up to the house and into the top room and I asked him. He said, 'Absolutely, no question. Yes, of course.' I was a little taken aback but I had to tell him that I didn't have a script yet so I didn't know what to offer him. He said it didn't matter. 'I'll walk across the screen, I'll read the telephone directory, I'll do whatever you'd like me to do. Of course I'll do it.' We discussed the project a little more and as I started to go he said: 'Dick, when you go to John and Ralphie tell them I'm doing it for Equity minimum'. The fact that he was prepared to do it for so little meant that when I went to anyone else, I was able to say this is the fee and it's the same fee that Larry is getting. We couldn't have made it without his offer. I was enormously grateful.

In its finished form *Oh! What A Lovely War* is a very political film. I didn't set out deliberately to politicise it but I tried to sharpen it a bit. I have to admit that in the final analysis it was not as good a film as the play; in the play there was an astringency which the film lacked. It was not my intention, that's what's so aggravating, but in the end result it was not as powerful in those terms. Emotionally, it was much more devastating because of the end shot and so on, which was my invention and had nothing obviously to do with the play whatsoever. I still don't know why it was but the idea, for example, that we had a cricket scoreboard with all the losses going up was simply too objective for some people. In the theatre, however, suddenly somebody walked across the stage with these massive losses hastily written on blackboards. The impact in the theatre was totally devastating and I still don't know quite why but the film was not as good.

For me one of the abiding sadnesses of *Oh! What A Lovely War* was that Len Deighton absented himself. He'd had a disagreement and he never confronted me with it so I don't really know what in fact it was all about. But he had this sort of blood-brother partner called Brian Duffy and they ended up having a terrible falling out. I don't quite know what the cause of it was, it may even have been what I was doing, I just don't know. But Len certainly wanted no part of it and indeed took his name off it. There was a great sadness in that because the idea and the manner in which it was transferred to the screen was not mine. I embellished it but it was a brilliant idea of Len's and I very much regret that he was not part of it. I think in a way he might have reined me back a bit. I am an emotional character and that tends to take me over sometimes and I think perhaps if Len had stayed on board he might have been a corrective.

Opposite: Laurence Olivier makes a point on *Oh! What A Lovely War*

Assembling the Crew

In 1969 Richard Attenborough's only aim as a director was to make his cherished film of the life of Mahatma Gandhi – 'Gandhiji' as he referred to him, using the Indian suffix 'ji' to indicate respect and affection. The path, however, would not be an easy one. From his first approach in 1962 by an Indian civil servant, Motilal Kothari, who had the original idea for the film, it would be 18 long years before the cameras finally started turning in earnest. But seven years after he had first decided he wanted to direct at least one movie he found himself directing *Oh! What A Lovely War*. Whether it was the allure of Len Deighton's script, whether it was the attraction of stamping his own vision on a piece of work, or whether it was simply and subconsciously the knowledge that a project like *Gandhi* was too big without some sort of rehearsal, Attenborough now found himself behind the camera for the first time.

The man who put him there was John Mills, one of his dearest friends and one of the greatest names in the British cinema. He had known, almost from the moment Attenborough first decided he wanted to do *Gandhi*, that the actor–producer wanted to become a director. And he felt that *Oh! What A Lovely War* was the project with which he could be tempted.

'Dickie always says that we decided we wanted someone who knew bugger all about directing, which is why we chose him,' recalls Sir John. 'But I was never in any doubt that he could direct a film and he would do a great job on this one. I think the idea first came to me during *Whistle Down the Wind*, which Dickie produced and his great friend Bryan Forbes directed. My daughter, Hayley, was in the film and it was based on a story by my wife. The film was so different and so imaginative that it was obvious in discussions with all of us that Dickie had had some creative input so perhaps he should do this script.'

Like most first-time directors, Attenborough knew what his film should

Attenborough's daughter Charlotte is now a successful actress. She made her debut in *Oh! What a Lovely War* and here her father tries to explain some of the finer points of film-making

look like on the screen. Getting that vision out of his head and into the camera was an entirely different prospect. He knew that if he was to realise his vision of Joan Littlewood's acclaimed musical he would need to have the best production talent in Britain. There was no point in having a stellar cast in front of the camera if they were going to be betrayed by inexperience behind it. So Attenborough set about assembling a crew who were among the best in their respective fields. The vital role of first assistant director went to Claude Watson, his cameraman was Gerry Turpin, his camera operator was Ronnie Taylor, Don Ashton was the production designer, Simon Kaye was the sound recordist, Kevin Connor the editor, and the music was in the hands of Alfred Ralston who had done the original show at Stratford East. Not only were these the best people available, they were also people with whom the neophyte director could work. He trusted and respected them and they admired him. This group also formed the basis of a creative nucleus who would go on to work with him many times more in the future.

However, the one person in whom perhaps Attenborough placed most trust was his long-time friend Ann Skinner. She was a continuity girl, or script supervisor as they are known in American productions. Most people with only a basic knowledge of the film industry assume that the function of the continuity person is to make sure the star is wearing the same tie in every shot

Gerry Turpin, Ann Skinner, Richard Attenborough and John Mills on *Oh! What A Lovely War*

or that his cigarette doesn't mysteriously change hands on screen. In fact that is the tip of the iceberg. A good continuity person can save a director's life time and time again by reminding him of what will and will not cut together by the time he gets to the editing room. Attenborough insists that he remains everlastingly grateful to Ann Skinner and the rest of the crew and would not have been able to do *Oh! What A Lovely War* without them.

'I always used to see myself as the agent of the cutting room on the studio floor,' says Ann Skinner, who is now a successful independent producer in her own right. 'This being a musical, it would be even more difficult to cut together but Dick understood about cutting to music which is something that a lot of directors don't, but he definitely did. I would give my opinion whenever he asked for it and he relied on it.'

Directors or actors will always tell you rather grandly that movie-making is a collaborative process. Generally they mean that if everyone collaborates with their way of thinking then everything will be just fine. However, *Oh! What A Lovely War* was a genuinely collaborative effort with Attenborough seeking and taking advice at every opportunity. But in any venture there can be only one boss.

'To me *Oh! What A Lovely War* still has the stamp of Dickie Attenborough all over it,' says Ann Skinner. 'When it came out I think it did receive a certain amount of criticism from those who had seen Joan Littlewood's production because it had such a pleasant and home-crafted quality about it. A lot of people fell in love with that but you couldn't put that on film. This movie, and maybe now *Shadowlands* in a different respect, was definitely an Attenborough film. He had to dream up how it was to be shot and I'm sure that if it wasn't actually his idea then he had the sense to grab it from whoever said, "Why not shoot it on the pier at Brighton?" He devised every scene and what people sometimes don't realise is that he is incredibly musical. He had the whole film virtually choreographed in his head before he started shooting.

'I was really sad about the way it was received in some quarters by people who knocked it for completely the wrong reason. There was no way that you could make this film the way that Joan Littlewood did the show. What I felt was marvellous was the way that Dick had made it accessible to an audience who would never have dreamed of going to see Joan Littlewood's musical on the stage. People like my parents saw it and adored it, but I don't think it quite found its audience and it got knocked because of that.'

Although he claimed then and still does now that at that time he knew 'bugger all' about directing films, Attenborough had made an inventive and striking début. In the light of that, his pleas of ignorance about the film-making process have a slightly disingenuous ring to them.

'He had produced all those films before *Oh! What A Lovely War*,' says Ann Skinner. 'He had fought with all those directors. He was an actor. Of course he didn't know bugger all about making films. Dick is a really canny person, how else could he and Bryan Forbes have produced the films they did? It's true that we were just coming out of what I call the "studio period" of making films in this country, which is why I think this was an even braver move on his part. In 1969 we were all used to making films in studios and not using locations. We were certainly not used to going on locations like Brighton rubbish dump and pretending it was the trenches instead of doing what we had usually done and finding a field that looks a bit like France. I can't honestly say where those ideas came from but basically I think Dick has rather an anarchic brain inside this straight, establishment exterior. That's what makes him so incredibly stimulating to work with.'

Sir John Mills had hoped that his old friend would rise to the challenge of the script and he recalls that he was not disappointed. 'Dickie is remarkably musical, which I think surprises a lot of people,' he says. 'I think he responded to that but he showed such imagination in the finished product. I knew that he was capable of realising the sort of picture we felt was in the script but I am bound to say that in some of the sequences he completely surpassed our expectations. He always seemed to know exactly what he wanted and he showed a doggedness in getting it. Like that extraordinary final shot with all of the crosses. They all had to be drilled into the Sussex Downs, thousands of them, but Dickie knew how stunning that scene would look on screen, and it did.'

One of the hallmarks of Attenborough's nine films as a director is his ability to draw from people performances of which they did not know they were capable. His secret is to treat them as individuals and encourage them to believe in the contribution they are making to the finished film. It's an attitude which has subjected him to scorn and ridicule over the years but no one can argue with the results he obtains.

'My first meeting with Dickie came right out of the blue,' recalls double-Oscar-winning sound recordist Simon Kaye. 'We were shooting *The Lion in Winter* at Ardmore studios in Ireland and we had a telephone call from Dickie's office to ask if it would be okay for him to come over and have a chat with me and Douglas Slocombe who was the director of photography. I had never met him, I never worked with him as an actor. But he came over and took an office in the studio for the day and we met when we came off the set when the day's shooting finished at six. As I say, I had never met him before but within minutes he was standing there in that office acting out *Oh! What A Lovely War* for us. He did zooms and he did tracking shots and he simulated crane shots and he was singing the songs and doing the dances. There was no doubt at all that he knew exactly what he wanted to do. This was a very exciting meeting for me because I was somewhat younger then and it struck me as a completely new approach. I had worked with Tony Richardson on *The Charge of the Light Brigade* the previous year and I didn't even meet him until the first day of shooting.

'That is the difference in the way different directors deal with people. I knew that I'd been recommended in both cases but as far as Dickie was concerned, he felt it was important for him to make a personal appeal. I did finally agree to do it but there were some problems in the negotiations and so on. But he wrote me the most beautiful letter thanking me because it would have been impossible, he said, to consider anyone else after he had met me and because of the rapport we had struck up. It is one of the most beautiful letters that I possess. But that is the sort of thing that Dickie does. It is the sort of thing that he is so very good at because it makes people feel wanted and needed.'

Simon Kaye's recollection of making *Oh! What A Lovely War* is of a process which became so collaborative that it almost resembled the collective approach to film-making. He remembers a group of about half a dozen key personnel who moved as though they were joined at the hip. 'Dickie is a great visualiser and he is very good at explaining what he wants,' Kaye continues. 'He'll spend ages. He'll go round the whole set explaining what he is trying to do just in case someone might say to him, "Wait a minute, it might be a good idea if we try such and such." Eventually I said to him, and this might have been a little cheeky but pretty much everything was done by committee on that shoot, so I didn't feel I was talking out of turn, "Don't you think you actually listen to too many people?" He thought for a minute and then he said, "I think I know what I want to do but if the carpenter comes along and says, 'Hey Dick, what do you think of this idea?' and I tell him to carry on knocking in nails then I may lose something of real value." That was a very interesting vision for any director to have of film-making and that was him at a very early stage. But I don't really believe him when he says he knew bugger all. He was a very good producer and if they're good at what they do then these sort of guys don't miss a lot. Dickie doesn't miss a thing. Even though he says he's deaf in one ear he hears everything that's going on.'

Attenborough could be as receptive to other people's advice as he chose to be but he knew that at the end of the day he would carry the can. If something didn't work on screen then no one was going to blame the carpenter for having a rotten idea instead of sticking to his own job. And when the chips were down he could stand his ground and insist on the shot he wanted, like that breathtaking closing sequence. That was the first shot that he thought of and he knew he had to have it. That's why, despite Don Ashton's objections, 15,000 holes were drilled for 15,000 crosses to be hammered into the Sussex Downs.

'Dick did sometimes lack confidence about what he wanted,' says Ann Skinner. 'That was one of the negative sides of him on *Oh! What A Lovely War*. He did actually know what he wanted, he just was not certain and he seemed to feel he had to test the ground all the time. Instead of saying, "Alright boys, over here on such and such a lens," he was more likely to say, "Well darlings, what about this on a such and such." The upshot was that you would end up with a discussion which I found to be sometimes a terribly frustrating exercise. But he always knew his own mind when it came to the actors. He knew what to do with the actors and that to me is the secret of making films. You can always find a good cameraman and a good operator. They'll decide what lens to use and how to light it if you're completely ignorant – which Dick wasn't – but if you can't handle the actors then you're sunk. Dick wasn't at all stupid or ignorant of the process, he just loves everybody around him to feel involved and feel that it is their project too. That's just him, that's the generous side of his nature.

'I don't think he chose the people he did on *Oh! What A Lovely War* through any lack of confidence. There was no suggestion that he needed these people to provide affirmation for his own decisions. I think he chooses people basically because he instinctively goes for the best and with his stature in the industry he would have been used to working with the best both as an actor and as a producer. I don't know that having his suggestions rubber stamped, as it were, is something that would have worried him. He was a first-time director and it was a big film. The first time you direct a movie it is different, and that doesn't mean to say that he didn't know anything about directing. As a producer he might have got used to telling people things but when you're directing everyone is constantly asking you questions all the time. There's also the process of watching the daily footage in the rushes and working out whether it will cut together, and also whether it will cut in the way you thought it was going to cut, which is quite a different thing. There are a lot more things to worry about when you are a director. I think that's why he chooses people who are good. He chooses them because he knows what they can do, he likes them as people and he can trust them to do what he hired them to do.

'When I gave up continuity and started producing I wanted him to do my first film, *Return of the Soldier*. He was just about to do *Gandhi* and he said he would do it if I would do *Gandhi*. I told him I was getting too old to wait that long because Gandhi had been on the go virtually since I first knew him. He had wanted me to do *A Bridge Too Far* before that but I said: "What's the point of having a continuity girl who closes her eyes every time there's a bang." So, very sadly and with floods of tears, I didn't do that. After that he said he missed having someone around who always told him the truth. At least if I thought

Attenborough demonstrates while Olivier and choreographer Eleanor Fazan look on during *Oh! What A Lovely War*

something was terrible I said it was terrible, and a lot of people don't I gather. Although there are a lot of directors who don't want to hear that anyway. Nevertheless, if you are there and your opinion is asked, I can't see the point of lying about it. If it's good you say it's good and if it's terrible you say it's terrible.'

So far Attenborough has worked with Simon Kaye more often than any member of his key production personnel. They have done six movies together and Kaye would go anywhere to make a film with him. One of the qualities which makes Attenborough so admired as a director by his production staff is his awareness and appreciation of what they actually do and how much they contribute to the finished film.

'A lot of directors do undervalue things like sound recording,' says Kaye. 'Dickie is very open and very warm and generous with his praise and appreciation. *Oh! What A Lovely War* was the first time we worked together but

I don't think we ever had a discussion about what he actually expected of me. He had hired me and he was trusting me to get on with my job. Only once did we discuss the specifics of a scene. Money was tight on this picture and I had to do a scene which involved a tracking shot of Laurence Olivier and Michael Redgrave in the back of an open-topped car. For that scene Dickie said to me, "You can have whatever you need to make this scene work. You can have all the equipment, you can have cars, trucks, everything, because I don't want to do any looping and anyway we wouldn't be able to afford it." Looping is the technical term for recording the sound in the studio afterwards and matching it to the film in post-production. We didn't have any other looping to do and it was going to cost £500 a day – and this was in 1969 – for Olivier and Redgrave to loop that one scene.

'The other thing with Dickie is that if you want something then you get it. If you tell him you need a proper track on certain scenes there are occasions when for perfectly good reasons he might ask if you could leave it and try to get it later, but in principle you get what you want. He wants quality from everyone in his movies and that is rare. American directors in particular often just want a guide track and will loop the sound later. I worked with Irving Kershner on the Bond movie *Never Say Never Again* and I told him that in one scene we were going to be in trouble with the background noise. However, I said with just a little more voice from the actors I thought we could get it.

'Kershner was taken aback and said, "I wasn't expecting this to be used."

'But I replied: "I was!"

'It's funny but Dickie and I never have those conversations. He knows we will get the best that is going and if I say I need a piece of sound to cover something or to fill in, then he knows the value of it. Even more so when you go to the dubbing theatre and spend six weeks there putting the track together, that's the time when if you haven't listened to the guy twiddling the knobs you're in trouble. You can still get it to work, but only with a great deal of time and money.'

In the final analysis *Oh! What A Lovely War* may simply have been the catalyst for a process which was inevitable. Whether it was for *Gandhi* or not, it seemed to be only a matter of time before Attenborough, who had already turned producer, took the final step and became a director.

'Retrospectively, I'm sure that's right,' says Ann Skinner. 'I don't think I was aware of it at the time or even thinking in those terms myself. When he called me to say he was directing his first picture I just thought it was terribly exciting for him. In hindsight, it wasn't such a leap. He was a hugely creative producer and he knew why everything was in the script and he passed an opinion on everything. He supported Bryan Forbes in those films and he obviously had a strong opinion about the movies. He wasn't a do-nothing producer, he was on the set every day, and I suppose on reflection it was a natural progression for him to become a director.'

Sir John Mills confesses he finds it a little difficult to talk about Attenborough as a director because he says everything he says about him ends up sounding like a paean of unalloyed praise. 'However, it is all true and I honestly mean it when I say that I believe he is a genuinely great director,' he insists. 'I've worked with Dickie many times as an actor – we first worked together on his début, *In Which We Serve* – and I think he is exactly the same as a director as he is as an actor. He doesn't change, no matter what side of the camera he is on. He is always honest, enthusiastic and very, very supportive.

'It's very difficult to sum up what it is that makes him such a great film-maker. I think there is his sense of vision, of course, but it is also his uncanny ability to work with actors. He is a great judge of acting, and he is able to inspire actors to great performances. He also has a marvellous eye for what is good in a performance. An actor knows that Dickie will print the best take and that is remarkably stimulating and encouraging in terms of producing your best work.'

Learning a Lesson

Young Winston was the first of the film biographies which people seem to think I do all the time. Making a film biography is a challenge for all sorts of reasons because invariably people will disagree with your interpretation of the character. It's one of the things people ask me about. Why must I take on such difficult projects? The honest answer is that I don't know but I think it may possibly be simply because all my life I've been much more interested in biography and history and so on than I have in fiction. I don't mean I don't read any fiction but given the choice I will read biography. I am simply fascinated by the way in which our lives are affected and moved and redirected in terms of other people's lives.

I believe that during each century or even each decade there are various figures, a number of people who, by virtue of their convictions – for evil or for good – actually change the course of history. They actually change the way in which we conduct our lives and indeed even affect us in terms of our relationships with one another. The people whose lives I have shown on screen – Winston Churchill, Mahatma Gandhi, Donald Woods, Steve Biko, Charlie Chaplin and C.S. Lewis – have all done that. They have all in some way or another nudged our attitudes, moved our vision and taken away the onion-skins over the eyes in terms of examining other people and attempting to find their susceptibilities, their frailties, and their strengths. That's what these biographical opportunities grant me. If, in addition to that, those people, such as Mahatma Gandhi or Steve Biko or indeed Churchill, actually changed the course of history then that is very exciting as well. So if you put all that together in varying forms I love the freedom and the opportunity granted to me to be able to spend the hours of the day doing something which really is a hobby, examining and looking and trying to understand periods of history and people within them. And when you consider I am also being paid to do

Richard Attenborough on *Young Winston*

it then it's just too good to be true.

You might say that there doesn't seem to be any obvious synergy between me as a Socialist and Winston Churchill, who is still remembered by a great many people as the man who turned the troops on the strikers. But you see again it is emotional. My impressionable years were obviously at the time just prior to and during the Second World War. In terms of my feelings about Franco and Mussolini – we tend always to think about Hitler but we should never ever forget those other two thugs and what they stood for – my feelings about that were very deep indeed. So too is my total revulsion in relation to everything they stood for. And, because of the way I felt, I hero-worshipped Churchill. It had nothing to do with his political standpoint. I believed passionately that Churchill to a certain extent single-handedly saved Europe. I don't care what has been written about him subsequently, there is little doubt in my mind that he saved Europe. He saved European civilization and he gave us our voice. Although the heart and spirit was there he, I believe, put words to it. Therefore he was a great hero and to that extent I was fascinated by what made up this man. And, rather like with Charlie Chaplin, I was fascinated to examine all those early years from the days when he was knee-high up to the time of his very first speech. I was, indeed I still am, in large measure influenced by my relationship with my own parents and I was captivated by the completely extraordinary relationship, or lack of it, that he had with his father, Lord Randolph Churchill. So with all of that and the *Boy's Own Paper* beginning to his career that he had in South Africa, I found it absolutely fascinating. It didn't worry me that he latterly became that figure as Home Secretary, that other aspect of him existed as such but I didn't worry about it. I saw it as something that needn't bother me too much because I wasn't dealing with it in this film. If I was dealing with Churchill and his whole career as such that would have been a very different movie. But I wasn't, it was limited up to the point of his first speech in the House of Commons and therefore that was my focus and that was my interest.

The offer that I originally received from Carl Foreman, the producer and screenwriter, was would I like to play Lord Randolph as well as direct. I made a mistake, I think. I would love to have done it but I didn't think I was really up to it. The part was eventually played, and played very well, by Robert Shaw. I was too convinced that directing and acting were separate. What I had learned from *Oh! What A Lovely War* was that directing was very difficult. Maintaining your objectivity so that you can make the best judgments throughout the film is relatively simple once you get to the stage of taking the film into the cutting-room, but during the actual shooting retaining that objectivity, although an absolute prerequisite, is much more difficult. In *Oh! What A Lovely War* I thought about the number of the scenes that I was attempting to direct. I also had an extraordinary mélange of people – there were quite a few who had never made a film before working alongside people who were the gods of their day, Richardson, Gielgud, Olivier and so on. I was immensely conscious of how difficult it was, especially in group sequences where you have to have eyes which are literally everywhere. To me, rightly or wrongly, bearing in mind what I had gone through in *Oh! What A Lovely War*, I thought that I would lose my objectivity if I was playing Lord Randolph as well as directing. In addition to that, Simon Ward was not Carl's first choice. I had fought like the clappers for him and I had battled to the point where I said, 'I'm sorry, it has to be Simon or . . . ' Having won that battle and got him there, he was then there to be shot at by anyone who cared to. I felt very strongly that my loyalty was to Simon and I felt that I needed to devote my entire concentration to him without worrying about a performance of my own.

The reason I was so keen on Simon was simply that I thought he was a marvellous actor with great physical agility. He had the ability, by virtue of his stage experience, to take on Churchill's persona dramatically and physically. Of course, it worked. Physically, when you looked at Simon, you could believe him as Winston Churchill. With hindsight, I regret not playing in the movie myself but I think it would have been unfair to have cast somebody who would either stand or fall by that performance for quite a number of years, then not to have my full concentration on his performance and so I didn't do it.

I'm sorry to say that my relationship with Carl Foreman on *Young Winston* was not always a happy one. It wasn't just the question of casting Simon: we disagreed on a number of things. I didn't think the interview sequences worked. We also disagreed on a number of major questions in the script, which

33

The glamour of stardom. Simon Ward shelters from the Welsh weather on *Young Winston*

meant that in some instances we actually shot alternatives because Carl didn't like my concept. Indeed, he persuaded me to re-cut the film in the end.

I believed passionately following *Oh! What A Lovely War* and on almost every other film I've done since then, that you cannot have an authority beyond the director. But I was very conscious of the fact that *Young Winston* was Carl's subject. Not only had he raised all the money, but he was the active producer day by day. There wasn't a single day when Carl wasn't there on the set. He was also the writer and with my innate reverence towards writers it seemed to me that I was engaged like a line producer, who is there to make sure things get done on time and on budget. I was in a way a line director. I could, and indeed I had to, accept the fact that it was Carl's subject and this is what Carl wanted. All I could do was to do my best to interpret it, which is what I did. Again, the

Carl Foreman and Richard Attenborough in one of their many discussions on *Young Winston*

evidence of my concentration and my reward and my quality, whatever quality I brought to it, was there in Simon, in Robert Shaw, in Anne Bancroft and many other wonderful performances. I got enormous satisfaction from that but at the end of the day I was doing certain things that I would have done another way because I bowed to Carl and I think properly so.

The experience of working with Carl Foreman on *Young Winston* strengthened my resolve to be my own boss if possible, there is absolutely no question of that. But my next two films were made for another man with a formidable reputation, Joe Levine. Joe, however, was not a producer, in the true sense of the word. Joe never criticised anything you did. He would be lavish in his praise and he would tell you that what you were doing would win every Oscar that was going. He was an impresario and in movie terms he was an executive producer. He came on the set when it suited him but he was not the controller of the picture, nor did he ever question a take or a set-up. That sort of arrangement was fine by me.

'This is all for you'

The man who would be Winston Churchill was discovered seducing a schoolteacher at the Theatre Royal in Haymarket. Simon Ward was playing 'a long-haired, incoherent lout' when he was spotted by one of Richard Attenborough's assistants who saw in him the potential to be the young Winston Churchill.

At this stage the 30-year-old actor was well established on the London stage although he had only a handful of film credits to his name. He made his début in Lindsay Anderson's controversial public-school movie *If...*, then went on to play Peter Cushing's accomplice in *Frankenstein Must Be Destroyed* for Hammer Films. His only other movie before *Young Winston* was *I Start Counting* about a young woman who believes her older brother may be a sex killer. None of these roles seems an automatic qualification to play Churchill and Ward himself admits it was quite a considerable leap of the imagination for the person who spotted him at the Theatre Royal. Ward was even more bemused because he hadn't been on any of the casting lists. Nonetheless, he went along to see Attenborough and producer-scriptwriter Carl Foreman in the belief that they might have wanted him to play the part of a junior officer.

'There were a couple of young officers at the end of one of the scenes in the script I had been given and I thought I was up for one of them,' Ward remembers. 'It was only when the interview had gone on for about three-quarters of an hour and I became aware of them walking around and staring intently at me that I realised the possibility that what they were talking about was the leading role itself. That came as a great shock and I felt ridiculous, absolutely ridiculous.'

The actor went back to the theatre that night and told his fellow cast members that he had been up for the part of Winston Churchill. Ward remembers the news being greeted with much hilarity all round. Then he was asked to go for a screen test which produced still more merriment among his colleagues. Ward at this stage shared their scepticism and refused to take the whole thing seriously. Even when he got the call back to do a second test he still wouldn't allow himself to get excited. His reasoning was that a second test meant there was still a great deal of doubt about whether or not he was up to it.

'Oddly enough, they used a lot of make-up on the first screen test, less on the second, and even less again on the third,' he recalls. 'But during that second test when I was in make-up I noticed there was a photograph of the young Churchill stuck up on the mirror as a guide. About halfway through the session I started to tell myself, "Yeah, you could do this. It's not as ridiculous as you thought it was." It was about then that I started to think that I would really rather like to do this because it was a rather good combination from my point of view. No one in their right mind would have turned down a film which opens with them sitting astride a white horse on top of a mountain with a magnificent vista unfolding beneath them. I decided that I really quite fancied the combination of the action stuff, which I'd always fancied myself doing, and the acting itself.'

That second screen test came and went with no decision. Ward was completely unaware of the behind-the-scenes battles going on between Attenborough and Foreman about the director's choice. He put it down to simple indecisiveness. There was a third test and by this time Ward admits he was feeling cheesed off by the whole process, which had now dragged on for three months. However, the third time was the charm and he ended up with the biggest role of his career and one which was to make him an international name.

Throughout the succession of tests no one had actually discussed with Ward how he would approach the part. The popular conception of Churchill is of the great statesman with a deep, resonant voice who sounded a lot like Richard Burton, a legacy of Burton having provided the voice-over for an acclaimed BBC documentary series on Churchill. Ward was aware that Churchill didn't really sound like the poor man's Burton but he also felt that, as far as his responsibility to the audience went, he would have to play to those conceptions, at least up to a point.

'The wonderful thing about Dickie,' he says, 'is that he would never talk about the generality of something, only the particular. There was never a time when we sat down and discussed the overall view of the characterisation. When we did sit down it was always about specific scenes and how we were going to play them.'

Ward is in no doubt that if his characterisation had not been what the director wanted then he would have been the first to hear about it. However, it is an Attenborough trait that he trusts the people he hires to do the job he hired them to do. Simon Kaye, his sound recordist from *Oh! What A Lovely War*, was with him again on *Young Winston*.

'I don't quite know what goes on between him and the actors before they arrive,' Kaye explains, 'but he is very trusting with the actors he chooses.

Attenborough, Simon Ward and Carl Foreman during Ward's final screen test for *Young Winston*

Obviously, if you're shooting on a far-flung location you might have one scene where you decide not to bring someone in to do it, and you can have the biggest problem in the world on that scene because you're not using a real actor. Even Dickie, with all the will in the world, sometimes can't get across what he might want the guy to do. Generally, though, he does get his point across to the actors, he doesn't always stand up and act it out necessarily, but he would if they wanted him to.

'On *Shadowlands*, for example, we had one day's shooting prior to the main shoot which involved a couple of little bits with Debra Winger and Anthony Hopkins. He'd already told me what he was expecting Debra to sound like in terms of her performance and the accent he was hoping she would play.

'I said to him, "How about Tony? What accent will he use?"

'He said, "I don't know."

Anthony Hopkins as Lloyd George and Richard Attenborough on *Young Winston*, the first of their five films together

'He genuinely didn't know and it didn't worry him because he trusted Tony to do what he was going to be paid to do.'

As well as Simon Ward in the title role, Attenborough had assembled a quality cast to support him. Robert Shaw would play Lord Randolph Churchill – the role originally offered to Attenborough – Anne Bancroft played Churchill's mother and dotted throughout the cast were names like Jack Hawkins, John Mills, Patrick Magee, Anthony Hopkins, and Edward Woodward. Ward's first dialogue sequence in the movie is with Shaw as his domineering father, a baptism of fire for any young actor. But films are generally not shot in chronological order so that scene didn't come until several weeks into the shoot. Whether by accident or design, the first scenes to be filmed were all action sequences so Ward would have a chance to find his cinematic feet by playing soldiers in the hills of South Wales which were doubling for Boer War South Africa.

'When we went to South Wales I was taken out on to the location on the first day,' he says. 'I walked up to the top of a hill with Dickie and we looked

Opposite: Anne Bancroft and Richard Attenborough between takes on *Young Winston*

down and we could see the railway line, we could see the engine, a bulldozer, a helicopter, and about 30 trucks. Dickie turned to me. "See," he said, "this is all for you." And we didn't shoot a single foot of film the whole week.

'It was raining and for that whole week we didn't film a thing. It was a desperate situation. Everything went wrong, the railway line collapsed, the locomotive broke down – it was simply an awful time. I began to think that the whole thing would have to be cancelled because it couldn't be done but we got through it and we started shooting the following week. I had six weeks in South Wales and that gave me the chance to get to know everyone on the unit. In certain situations one has inevitable self-doubts as an actor which I don't think people take seriously enough. Certainly directors seldom take it seriously enough to consider how nervous and unsure of themselves actors are when they walk on to a set on the first day. After you've been working for a long time you do often know other people, even though you may not have seen them for a while. Initially, though, they all know each other and you are an outsider. Coupled with one's own innate self-doubt that can make things terribly difficult and that's where Dickie was wonderful. Not just with me but throughout the shoot. People would come in to do a couple of lines and Dickie would greet them, welcome them, talk to them, and introduce them around the set as though they were his oldest friend. The unkind see that as often being over-affectionate. I always saw it as a wonderful tool to make an actor feel at home.

'When I look back on *Young Winston* now I wonder if I needed a little cossetting, I don't think I did. I do know I needed all the help I could get and welcomed it but I would have hated it if I thought that I was being somehow sheltered. I was an unknown film actor but I wasn't an unknown theatre actor. I'd done a lot of work and I thought I was quite a success. I certainly felt then that I knew what I was doing in a way that I don't any more as the abysses of angst have deepened over the years. For those first six or seven weeks I was just running around and doing it and doing it and doing it and the first time I went to see the rushes I was in total despair. I'd never seen rushes before – those are the hastily printed versions of that day's takes. We had worked very hard together on it and I thought I was getting somewhere with it but when I saw the first week's rushes I was shocked. It wasn't Winston Churchill on the screen at all; it was me, and it looked ridiculous. I thought I'd made this great imaginative leap and I was going to see this different person. Not at all; it was me all along.

'I don't recall feeling any pressure because of that, I think some self-defence mechanism leaped into place. I was terribly aware of the responsibility but because of Dickie's support I always felt it was going to be alright.'

There is one defining moment for the audience in *Young Winston*. It is the moment when, despite his initial alarm at those rushes, Simon Ward 'becomes' Winston Churchill, or at least the Winston Churchill of popular perception. Young Winston has returned from the Boer War as a hero and is being debriefed about his experiences. During the course of the interviews he begins the transformation from the ambitious, arrogant young man into the future prime minister and world leader. The scenes worked for Carl Foreman, they

Opposite: Lifelong friends. Attenborough and John Mills on the set of *Young Winston*

Richard Attenborough and John Mills discuss a scene in *Young Winston*

worked for the audience, but Attenborough was never really happy with them. And neither was Simon Ward.

'It was just me and three cameras and they were frightfully difficult scenes to do,' he remembers. 'There was a stylistic jump and I'm not sure that they worked. Somehow the story seemed to stop for a time. It was one of the scenes they had done for the screen test so I knew the words but obviously one felt dreadfully exposed as one would in a real interview. A lot of the dialogue was in Churchill's own words so the cadences and the sounds made one go in that particular direction. I remember watching the rushes and the clapper-board came in and went out. Before the board came in I was talking to Dickie who then disappeared behind the camera. The board came in and Dickie left it a few moments before saying, "Action" and the most extraordinary thing happened. In that time my face actually changed to resemble Churchill. Somehow or other something had changed in my face. I hadn't done that, it was a product of my state of mind and Dickie had wrought it.'

After filming *Oh! What A Lovely War* on exotic locations like Brighton rubbish-dump, *Young Winston* took Attenborough for the first time to the spectacular locations which were to become a trademark. In *Young Winston*

Morocco doubled for the Sudan for the spectacular scenes of the Battle of Omdurman, in which the young Churchill found himself an exhilarated participant. The locations were far-flung but that proved an unexpected bonus for sound recordist Simon Kaye.

'Some of those Moroccan locations were so remote that we couldn't bring a generator near them, we had to run cables,' he recalls. 'At least that meant we didn't have the common location problem of generators running in the background. We did have some problems with the action scenes because they obviously present you with their own unique difficulties. You have loads of horses, foreign actors, crowds that don't understand what we are doing and why we want them to be quiet for a minute, half a minute would do sometimes. These are the problems that you fight and you battle with but they don't really involve the director. It's usually the first assistant who has that particular battle.'

The Battle of Omdurman is principally famous for being the last cavalry charge by British troops. For Simon Ward it brought home a legacy of that long and frustrating screen-testing process. The scenes required Churchill to be in the thick of the fray and a double could not easily be used. So inevitably he was asked the classic audition question: 'Can you ride?' He replied with the classic actor's answer, which is always in the affirmative whether you can or not. In Ward's case he could ride although he hadn't for some time. 'When I gave the classic reply I was met with the very unclassic response of: "Right, we're going out to Harrow next week so we'll see you on a horse." I hadn't ridden for 13 years but we went out to this stable and I got up on the horse and everything was alright. Then they put up jumps which absolutely horrified me and I pointed out I never actually said I'd done that. They were quite happy because the riding sequences weren't until the end of the picture which was four months away so they would bring a horse out to Shepperton for me so that I could ride every day. Then they discovered I wasn't insured for that. The insurance company wouldn't let me practise riding in a field at Shepperton, they would only allow me to get on a horse in front of 300 Moroccan cavalry extras filming the charge at Omdurman.'

It was during those scenes in Morocco that Simon Ward first became aware that, in some respects, Attenborough's talents as a director were being wasted. The scene of the military convoy, which opens the movie, took hours to set up. Work started at six in the morning and they were lucky to actually get the shot by mid-afternoon. If the shot didn't work then it would take four hours to get everyone into position to do it all over again. 'What would Dickie be doing while this was going on?' asks Ward rhetorically. 'All he could do was stand around and wait while other people made sure that 200 bullocks were in the right place. That's absolute nonsense and in many ways a waste of his talent. I think Dickie is desperately undervalued as a director and that's why I wish he had done more films like *Shadowlands* where people can appreciate how good he really is with actors.'

For Simon Ward, Attenborough's greatest gift is his ability to actually see what's going on. This, he says as a veteran now of more than 20 films and countless plays, is not necessarily a common trait in directors. 'Dickie is so superb at looking at what's happening,' says Ward with genuine admiration. 'Film directors on the whole, I believe, either don't look or if they do they are simply unable to tell the difference between what an actor is doing in take one and take four. Maybe they just don't know what it is that they want and therefore don't say anything and don't assist in bringing out the character. They only seem to be interested in what's going on in the background. *Young Winston* was the "most epic" of the films I've done but I have done other big action films and the directors always seem to be looking at what's going on with the house on fire in the top-right-hand corner of the screen, rather than looking at what the actors are doing in the foreground. When I pay money to go to the cinema what I'm looking for is what is actually happening between those two people in the foreground. Of course that background action is important but it's not the vital thing. Dickie always watches what's going on in the foreground and has wonderful people like David Tomblin to concentrate on what's happening in the background.'

'It's not true to say that he does this simply because of his experience as an actor. It's not always the case that actors who turn directors are good at handling other actors. In terms of handling actors sometimes it's the actor turned director who appears with the longest, most vicious whip in his hand and treats everyone badly to get his own back for all the years of humiliation he has suffered.'

As a theatre director himself, Ward knows the temptations that exist. A director reads a script and knows in his head how those lines are going to sound as delivered by his cast. The problem is how to get this optimum sound out of the director's head and into the actors' mouths without alienating the actor by actually giving them line readings.

'Dickie manages to do this with a combination of wooing and trust,' says Ward admiringly. 'You learn to trust him implicitly. If he had told me to stand on my head and cluck like a chicken because it had to happen at this particular moment in the script then I would have done it because I trusted him. As an actor I have a feeling of what I want to do but I love being told. Most actors like to be told if they have faith in the person doing the telling. It's the worst feeling in the world to be told to do something if you know the man's a sham. That's no good at all and as you get more experience you find ways of resisting that. But Dickie has an enormous empathy with actors and that's one of the things that makes him such a great director.'

Filming is Living

I did *A Bridge Too Far* because of three men: Joseph Levine, William Goldman and Mahatma Gandhi. I was still trying to get *Gandhi* made and at the end of 1974 had gone to Los Angeles for talks with Warner Brothers. While I was in Los Angeles Joe Levine invited me to his luxurious suite at the Beverly Hills Hotel where he told me, in no uncertain terms, that I was wasting my time. 'You'll never get that picture made without me,' he said, or words broadly to that effect. 'Why don't you do this instead,' he said, gesturing to a copy of Cornelius Ryan's *A Bridge Too Far* which was on a coffee table. The understanding was that if I did this picture then Joe would help me to make *Gandhi*.

Even with *Gandhi*, I'm not sure that I would have done *A Bridge Too Far* until I met William Goldman. I think it was Bill's creative juices which resulted in me getting involved. I have always had the most profound respect for the writer in the process of movie-making. A good script is an absolute prerequisite because of the ideas, the concepts and so on. If you do not have it on the page in the screenplay then you simply cannot have it on the screen in the movie. You can bugger up a marvellous screenplay but you can't create something out of nothing yourself. There were enormous problems with the structure of *A Bridge Too Far* because of the complexity of the story. But I do remember coming out of Bill's office in New York and almost dancing down Park Avenue. The whole of one wall was covered in a sort of green felt to make a giant bulletin board. On that board Bill had worked out the activities of the five nationalities involved; the British, the Americans, the Germans, the Dutch and the Poles. They were all written on a series of index cards. Then he would take a card down and add it to another pile or put it back in its original place because it didn't work there, and so on. Watching him create this was, in fact, like watching the Allied Supreme Commander conducting his

47

operations. It was extraordinary but he is a wonderful fellow.

One of the buggers of film criticism is that you can have someone like Bill who is so good, so clever, and so ingenious that in the final analysis his skills are almost totally overlooked. It's rather like a situation I encountered recently with my brother David who has approved of the things I've done – often very warmly – but has never ever written to me before about a movie. But he wrote to me about *Shadowlands*. He said he had enjoyed it and then he went on to talk about the music of George Fenton who does the music for David's own natural-history series on television. He said it was the most extraordinary thing because it must have been an hour or more before he took any notice of the music. He then realised, of course, for that hour he had been listening to film music but it had never registered as such. In other words the spirit of the music and the mood George had created with it was so perfectly judged that it wouldn't get good reviews because you didn't know it was there. It was an essential part of the work, totally integrated, which is almost the whole point. It is exactly the same with good screenwriting. *A Bridge Too Far* was probably the most complex story you could ever conceive of but instead of praising what Bill had achieved you get these arseholes who say things like: 'Oh, I thought having the Poles there was a total diversion'. They simply have no concept of how difficult it was to pull something like that together. This is a prerequisite of factual content which simply cannot be ignored.

That complexity in terms of plot and having so many stories interwoven was one of the reasons why I was in favour of having our all-star cast. Joe Levine wanted one too but for entirely different reasons. Joe believed that because the budget was going to be very significant – around $23.5 million – the only way to make that work in terms of getting his money back was to spend a similar amount more on the cast. They were commanding almost unbelievable amounts – Robert Redford got $2 million. This was seen by Joe as a gamble which he hoped would eventually enable him to recoup the massive sums already invested. I wanted stars but simply in recognition of the complexity of the script and the relationship of those five strands, one to another. I thought if you had Sean Connery in charge of one operation and James Caan very much out there on his own, and Tony Hopkins as Colonel Frost, with Gene Hackman as the Polish commander, then even if they were all in khaki or all in tin helmets people would say, subconsciously, 'I recognise Sean Connery', or, 'I recognise Michael Caine.' Therefore, at a basic level they could still follow all of their individual stories. But once again in came the knockers with their claims about star-spotting and two-and-a-half-hour peepshows.

I had the same thing in *Shadowlands* where they made a great fuss about Joy Gresham's remission period. I was absolutely screaming with fury at those silly buggers who said: 'Why can't they get their facts right? The remission period was six years or whatever it was – it appeared no more than six months in the film. I expect they wanted that little boy there at the end and that's why they did that.' You do almost get beside yourself with comments like that. You

Opposite: Screenwriter William Goldman and James Caan relax between takes on *A Bridge Too Far*

Attenborough and James Caan on *A Bridge Too Far*

want to say: 'How do you in fact deal with that if you have built up an audience's interest in a character or a person? What do you do? Do you re-cast for the last and biggest scene in the whole movie and utterly destroy the whole dramatic shape? Or perhaps we should have put a moustache on a nine-year-old boy? What do you do? I'm afraid that sort of attitude entirely defeats me, I simply do not understand it.

There is one position in the film industry which doesn't have anything like the attention it ought to have and that is the job of first assistant director. I was blessed on *A Bridge Too Far* by having the man who is the best in the business, David Tomblin. If you are an auteur, totally conscious and aware and sufficiently experienced to rely on your own judgment then that's one thing. I, however, am not an auteur. In a way, if it's not too fanciful, I am like the conductor of an orchestra. The score is there in the form of the script, and the various departments in the production are like the various sections of the

Attenborough and David Tomblin plot the logistics of another action scene in *A Bridge Too Far*

orchestra, the massed strings are in one place, the brass section in another and the woodwinds, etc. in their own places. The conductor holds together all those various forms and he permits now and again the flute solo or the trumpet solo or the first violin solo or whatever. But the person who organises the orchestra, who brings that orchestra together on the floor and takes care of all the requirements of the shooting floor is the first assistant director. He's not there for the production designer, or the costume director or the editor or the lighting cameraman or anyone else in a fundamentally creative position; he doesn't have anything to do with them, he brings the working floor together. I would have to say that when I did eventually embark on *Gandhi* I would not have even tried it without David Tomblin. He is unequivocally the best first assistant in the world. If it was left up to him Steven Spielberg, for example, would rather never make a movie than not have David. He can't have him always but that would be his wish. David Tomblin in terms of teaching me how you organise and how you marshal large crowds and huge action sequences is unique. Just consider the sequence on the bridge where Tony Hopkins and his men are dug in and defending against German attack. You can imagine the extent of the organisation of that, of all the special effects, of all the gunfire effects, of all the trick camerawork and the various crashes which all have to take place at the same time and in the correct order. Those sort of tuition sessions which I went through in *A Bridge Too Far* really allowed me to dare in *Gandhi* to use crowds and numbers in scenes like the funeral procession where we had 400,000 people. I don't think even David could ever actually have done it without the experience of *A Bridge Too Far*.

Some people say it's almost like two films going on at the same time with David looking after the background and me looking after the foreground. To a certain extent that is true and to a certain extent it is the only way you can do it on films as big as *A Bridge Too Far* or *Gandhi* or *Cry Freedom*. What I simply do not understand are directors who are able to go off the set and watch the scene on a tiny little monitor and decide what the ultimate shape and form of that sequence will be, or indeed their choice of one take over another. Ultimately, the eyeball, which is the size of a pinhead on that ridiculous little monitor, is six foot across on the screen. Everything you see in relation to your foreground is absolutely vital to the eye. In any event, you can't watch a take through the viewfinder while you're watching other things, you've got to look, you've got to see. So that synergy between me and David, the meshing of foreground and background, is absolutely vital. If you find yourself working with a first assistant who doesn't understand what you want from a scene or indeed what you believe ought to be the impact of the overall background contribution to the foreground then you're in terrible trouble. The wonderful thing about David is that he has such confidence in his own ability that you can say, 'It doesn't work, David.' Only once have I ever had a row with him which was when he thought the second-unit priorities were impinging on the first unit on the station scene in *Chaplin*. Oh, he was angry at me because I had said something that upset him but I have never really had a fundamental disagreement with David. He is unique. He is extraordinary

Sean Connery looks on as Richard Attenborough makes his point on *A Bridge Too Far*

and tireless in his commitment. But at the same time the lovely thing is that this great bull-necked tough is, in fact, a total softie. The result is that the crowds who move on our units in total fear and trembling of David's wrath know that at the end of the day they will be justly dealt with. They know that if there is a concern they have only to place a situation before David where compassion is required and he is a pushover.

I had 15 big names in the cast of *A Bridge Too Far*, including superstars like Robert Redford and Sean Connery, but I was never too worried about clashes of ego or temperament. I had a feeling from experience that there would be no trouble. The only scene I had the tiniest bit of doubt about was the opening scene in Browning's headquarters where we had Sean Connery, Dirk Bogarde and Ryan O'Neal together. I was a little concerned but I took some comfort from my own similar experience as an actor in *The Great Escape*. In that movie you had the Americans represented by Steve McQueen, James Coburn, Charles Bronson and James Garner and we presented James Donald, Gordon Jackson, Donald Pleasance and Angus Lennie and me. We were all good actors but we had no one who was remotely comparable to those big boys, although, with the exception of Steve, they weren't such big stars at that stage. James Garner, for example, was still on television and Charles Bronson still had to make his big break. But they knew how the British cultivated actors, they knew that we possessed Olivier, Richardson, Gielgud, Guinness, Redgrave and so on. They also knew that no British actor ever threw a tantrum, that nobody ever gave a bugger about the size of their caravans and so on because they were repertory players. Olivier might be doing *Othello* one night and four lines in Congreve the next night, so that sort of stupidity was not part of the repertory tradition. Indeed that awareness actually resulted in Steve and the others acknowledging a kind of respect for us which was almost reverence and slight apprehension that we could do it and they couldn't. Now by the time I came to do *A Bridge Too Far* I knew that. I knew perfectly well that 25 years later if you put Ryan O'Neal next to Dirk Bogarde or to Sean Connery or for that matter to Olivier or Liv Ullman that they just didn't want to behave stupidly and they didn't. So there wasn't a tantrum or a show of petulance from any of them.

At the end of *A Bridge Too Far* I was more exhausted than I think I have ever been in my life. I took to my bed and slept for four days, waking only for meals. The physical pressure involved in making this film was awful, it was the worst of all. On *Gandhi* we were on our own in large measure. Apart from the funeral sequence which was filmed on the Raj Path we could do pretty much what we wanted. Over and over and over again on *A Bridge Too Far*, however, there were all sorts of other constraints. Nobody had ever closed the Nijmegen Bridge, for example, since the war and we had an enormous battle to get them to agree to do it. Then they said, 'That's it, if you don't do it in that time then you don't have it.' I know that for *Gandhi* we had three-hour drives to locations in the back of beyond in those vehicles with bald tyres and then we'd come back and be told there was a question in Parliament about the movie the following day. So you'd have to prepare answers so ministers could be briefed then you would perhaps have an hour of crowd casting. If it was a rushes day and there was footage to be viewed you might be sitting there until two or three in the morning. That was tiring and physically draining but what I mean about *A Bridge Too Far* is that the nervous energy required a special strength. When you had Bob Redford who cost $2 million and his overage – the penalty clause in his contract, if you like, if he is kept beyond the agreed date – was half a million a day, that was terrifying.

Is any film worth that kind of pressure? Of course. For me filming is breathing and living . . . Being alive.

When Dickie Whistles

T he Million Dollar Hour has passed into movie mythology. The hour in question started at eight o'clock on the morning of 3 October 1976, a Sunday, and the location was Nijmegen Bridge in the Netherlands.

With only three more days to go, filming on *A Bridge Too Far* was almost over but this was one of the most crucial scenes in the movie. It involved Robert Redford, arguably the biggest movie star in the world at that time, as the American Major Julian Cook leading his troops in their part on the assault of Nijmegen Bridge. The local authorities had given permission for the use of the bridge for one hour only between eight and nine on three successive Sunday mornings. Sunday 3 October was the last of those Sundays. Along with the rest of the crew Redford would be paid off the following Wednesday. If they didn't get the shot then they would have to pay him and the other hundreds of people involved on the shot until the following weekend, if they could get permission to shoot on the bridge again. Since the original permission took the better part of a year to organise no one was particularly keen to try that again. The shot had to work, it was as simple as that.

It was Oscar-winning screenwriter William Goldman who actually coined the phrase 'the Million Dollar Hour' in his excellent book *Adventures in the Screen Trade*. He said then and he agrees now that a million dollars was probably on the low side. The pressure on Attenborough was intense.

'You must understand that in commercial terms Dickie had two flops going into this,' explains Goldman. 'He was lucky to have the job and this was a giant movie. It had the biggest budget of any movie ever up to that point. I think it was something that he really wanted to do and it was a real break that he had it. If the picture had gone badly, if it had gone over budget, if there had been troubles with it, his career might have effectively ended before it got started. As wonderful as they were, the first two movies hadn't really broken out; they

were commercial failures and this movie was not meant to be a commercial failure. There was terrible pressure on him basically to make the movie work and make it work within the conditions he was given.'

Goldman recalls Attenborough whistling as if to reassure everyone as he dealt with the last-minute enquiries and problems from his faithful crew as the fateful hour approached. He relied enormously on his first assistant director, David Tomblin. Attenborough and Tomblin have since formed a formidable partnership but this was their first outing together. If Goldman had known then what Tomblin knows now he might have seen things a little differently.

'When Dickie whistles you know you've got problems,' says Tomblin. 'He's feeling the pressure when he whistles and once he starts you know you have to think about things a little more. However, he is the epitome of grace under pressure and even under the most extreme strain he is never anything less than a gentleman.'

Tomblin recalls every day of *A Bridge Too Far* as having its own particular kind of pressure. With parachute drops, aeroplanes, gliders, tanks and explosions to organise on a daily basis there was no such thing as an easy day. The image of Attenborough as a general waging his own private military campaign is one which has been used often but seldom with more justification than in this case.

'Nijmegen Bridge is like the M1,' says Tomblin, 'and you can only shut it down for three or four minutes at a time. You are also controlling the river traffic which is a bit like the River Thames. When you've got all that going on then you have to get it right each time. Then you have to clear all the roadblocks away and let the traffic flow and then you've got to do it all again.'

Attenborough's relationship with David Tomblin borders on the uncanny. The director is small, outgoing, with enormous amounts of energy. His first assistant is a large, taciturn former Marine whose bark is much worse than his bite. At times in films like *A Bridge Too Far* or *Gandhi* it's as if there are two complementary movies occupying the same screen. Working on 'Bridge' and again on *Chaplin*, William Goldman got a keen sense of the relationship between these two very different men.

'David is as good as it gets at what he does,' he says with genuine admiration. 'What nobody really appreciates is that the shooting of a film, which is actually the middle third of the production process, is the most chaotic and that is generally when the press are around so they get all of these misconceptions. What David does is to smooth the waters so that the others around him can do their work. He's not supposed to soothe the actors, he's not supposed to make sure the sets look pretty; his job is to make sure that everything is running smoothly so that everyone else can get on with their jobs.

'Dickie tends to work with the same people from picture to picture whenever possible. They tend to be very nice, just as he is very nice. Dickie is not explosive and I don't think he likes a lot of explosive people around him. Some directors thrive on that, they love chaos and argument and things. That doesn't mean they're wrong, that's just the way their motor works best. Dickie tends not to, I think in part because he is so goddam English. The whole trick

Opposite: Setting up a shot on *A Bridge Too Far*. Attenborough is on top of the camera position. Elliot Gould, one of his stars, is in the foreground

of Attenborough is that I've always maintained he has the wrong body shape. He should look like Henry Fonda, he should be gaunt and slim and use up lots of energy. The fact is that he is cherubic and that look doesn't go with his energy.'

If Richard Attenborough was ever going to become explosive on the set then *A Bridge Too Far* would not have been the time to do it. He had 15 big names in his cast, five of whom – Robert Redford, James Caan, Ryan O'Neal, Sean Connery and Gene Hackman were genuine superstars of that period. At $23.5 million he had the biggest budget ever committed to a movie at that time. And he had to deal with one of Hollywood's most mercurial producers.

Joseph E. Levine was the last of the old school of movie tycoons. Ferociously independent, he knew the value of a buck and he was one of the greatest showmen in the movies. He made his name on *Hercules* in 1959. Levine acquired the American rights to this truly awful Italian epic, starring Steve Reeves, for $120,000. He then took the unheard-of step of advertising his movie on television, which was at that time being held responsible for the collapse in movie attendances. The results were staggering. Before the audience had time to work out just how bad this movie was, it had grossed $20 million. That's a respectable total for an imported movie these days; in 1959 it was *Jurassic Park* business. Levine had shown his eye for the main chance back in his early days in the business when he was exhibiting three-reelers. In those days you could hire the movie for a day, screen it, and then pay the renter. Levine hit on the idea of having three staggered performances at three separate venues. The shows started at half-hour intervals and when reel one finished at the first theatre it was then delivered to theatre two by a man on a bike. Once it had run there it went on to theatre three and so on. The result was that Levine got three times the revenue for the same rental fee.

He brought that same acumen to the production of *A Bridge Too Far*. By assembling a cast of huge names with broad international appeal he could sell off the foreign rights in advance. The scheme was so successful that the film actually went into profit before it had finished shooting. The success of Levine's tactic, however, meant that the film was committed to a specific delivery date, which meant that Goldman was actually still trying to write a script based on Cornelius Ryan's massive tome while the sets were being built. The fact that they didn't know exactly what he was writing only added to the problems because Goldman was by his own admission having enormous problems finding a cinematic structure.

'I don't like to show people things,' says Goldman of his working style. 'A lot of people who know about these things don't actually want to read scripts in the middle. You have no sense of the sweep of the film or where it is going. I may have a very dumb scene in the first half but the reason it's there is that it pays off in the second half. If you don't have the second half to hand then you don't know that. I have a memory that everyone was under terrible pressure because they were building and no one had seen the script. My memory is of Dickie coming out of the room where he had read my draft and he was sobbing. We embraced and I knew we were on our way. We were already into the budget

Joe Levine, William Goldman and Richard Attenborough on *A Bridge Too Far*

but the script was alright. I'd never had that situation before, where they were building while I was writing.

'Joe Levine's money was the one thing overlaying the whole production. Almost 20 years ago we were talking about the biggest budgeted movie ever made – not the most expensive but the one with the biggest original budget. It was $23.5 million then, so I would guess that would put it in the $60 million category now. That's *Last Action Hero* territory but even that movie was made with the backing of a major studio, so that was the bank's money. This was Joe Levine's money – he was the bank and that made for a lot of pressure.'

In that sort of situation you could have no better ally than Richard Attenborough. David Tomblin maintains Attenborough plays movie politics better than anyone. 'He is absolutely brilliant,' he says admiringly. 'I barely have the time and energy to make the film; he has the time to make the movie

Gene Hackman inspects Sean Connery's swing during the filming of *A Bridge Too Far*

and get involved in the politics, and how he does it is beyond me. He knows everybody's name. I don't, I forget my own half the time when we're shooting. He is great, but then he is also an actor. Even when he is directing he's an actor. I always know when there's a camera around because he changes, he shows off. Dickie loves to show off and that's why he's an actor.'

Attenborough's skill as an actor is an undoubted asset when he is dealing with his cast but it also pays dividends with his crew and the studios. Whistling while waiting for the Million Dollar Hour to begin may have been one of the finest performances of Attenborough's career but there were only 275 people there to see it. But if even one of them had failed to be convinced, then panic could have spread through the set like wildfire. His acting abilities also enhance his natural diplomacy which has been continually tested over the years, especially when working with Joe Levine.

There are three major operations in *A Bridge Too Far*. There is the attack on the bridge by Redford's men, there is the land assault by Anthony Hopkins's

Robert Redford and Richard Attenborough on *A Bridge Too Far*

Colonel Frost, and before that there is the massive parachute jump which initiated this bold strategic coup which was designed to end the war prematurely. For each of the three operations there was a massive planning meeting which involved every aspect of Attenborough's forces. David Tomblin played a key part in planning for every eventuality. 'When you've got as many cameras as we had you're not going to walk around being specific in your shots. You know basically what you are going to do and then you have to trust the people you employ. All you can do is tell them to get in amongst it and get the best shots they can. One particularly brilliant cameraman was Peter MacDonald. For the actual attack on the bridge we had nine cameras and we did the whole thing in four days, which was right on schedule. After every take Peter and I would rush about the set. He moved nine cameras and I reorganised so that for every take we had nine more shots. People with that kind of attitude contribute an enormous amount.

'For the parachute jump we were very lucky. We didn't have bad weather as such but there were other problems. The first time we did it they landed in the wrong place and missed the area completely. The next drop was particularly tense because, as I remember it, we had 800 people on the ground with parachutes and

22 cameras – 11 in the air and 11 on the ground. We had to co-ordinate the drop so that as the guys were coming down the people on the ground would get their chutes up in the air so that when the two met it looked like they had just landed. If you're too late they all blow away, and if they're too early they're all standing there with collapsed parachutes. So those things were a great pressure, especially as the shoot and the night wore on. They had to stay out there all night and we had to devise a system of feeding people without moving them, collecting all the garbage and attending to all their other requirements.'

The parachute drop was duly filmed. David Tomblin was right about the weather; it wasn't bad. The light was, however. Neither of the two days had what Attenborough wanted. They were okay but they were not up to his standards. That meant it had to be done again but that would involve still more money. Attenborough made the call to Levine who was in hospital recovering from surgery. By chance, William Goldman had dropped by to see how the producer was doing.

'I remember when Dickie called and said he wanted to shoot the scene again, and on a Saturday, and Levine was screaming down the phone at him. Dickie apparently told him: "It will not be magical with what we have, we need the sun." And Levine asked: "Are we going to get the sun tomorrow?" Attenborough presumably said he couldn't make any promises but he thought they might and the British paratroopers had said they would do the drop. Finally, Levine asked what it was going to cost and I think the answer was about $75,000. Now you have to understand that this is his money and they already had the scene. Levine finally said, "Oh, fuck you, do it!" And all of the material that you see in the finished film is from that Saturday shoot because Attenborough got the sun. No studio would have done that, it was an absolute fortune, but Levine did it. And I think one of the reasons he did it was because of Dickie. He was the only person who could talk to Levine, he knew exactly how to handle him.'

If Attenborough was able to handle the mercurial Levine then he was no less able to handle his cast of stars and superstars. With 15 names, all listed alphabetically for fear of arguments over billing, there was the potential for some catastrophic clashes of egos and personalities but none of this ever came to pass. David Tomblin recalls getting an extra pair of hands when he was moving his roadblocks on Nijmegen Bridge – they belonged to Robert Redford who was so aware of the pressure that he pitched in with the crew to make sure everything got done. As a veteran chronicler of the whims and vagaries of high-priced acting talent, William Goldman was as surprised as anyone by the behaviour of people who, in the wrong circumstances, could happily argue for days about the size of their trailer or the amount of their walking-around money.

'I thought the stars behaved remarkably well,' he recalls. 'Stars tend to need tending, they want that, they need it, they expect it. They want to be cuddled and told that they're loved and all that nonsense. The whole trick is that we all want that and what shocks us about stars is that they are so beautiful. We've seen them on film, we know how efficient they are, they can handle any situation. But when you're in a work situation and see them panic, that can be pretty unnerving. Everyone expects me to panic because I'm a writer so of course I'm neurotic, but stars aren't because they are sublime and when they panic, boy! Stars are a problem and everyone knows that, but they were not on this picture.

'One of my very strong memories is that we cut at the end of one scene and went to another set-up. As we cut I remember Dick grabbing a piece of heavy equipment and lugging it to the new set-up. I remember thinking how professional the whole thing was. I think the stars behaved because they felt no pressure on themselves. If the movie was a stiff it wasn't any of their specific faults. They were all in it together and they were jobbed in and jobbed out for two weeks and gone and they got a pile of money for their efforts. There was no room for any egos because there was no time for any egos because of the way the production was set up. If we're late with Star B then Star C is screwed up so my memory is that there was zero ego on that set, no one had any trouble.'

The shooting of *A Bridge Too Far* was completed on time and on budget. The consequences for Attenborough were a bout of devastating exhaustion but also a film that was already a hit, a movie which was in profit before it hit the cinemas. The response to the film was enthusiastic everywhere except America. Most critics praised Attenborough for having constructed a passionately anti-war film within the framework of a conventional war movie. The Americans were less easy to convince. They focussed on things like what they perceived to be Ryan O'Neal's youth in playing General James Gavin, even though O'Neal was the same age as Gavin, who was the youngest general in the American Army. William Goldman remains saddened but philosophical.

'A lot of people will say to me now: "I saw that movie on television and it was really good." I didn't look at it for a great many years because I was so disappointed at the reaction it got. It did very well around the world and made a lot of money for a lot of people but it was basically not what I thought it would be in the United States. I thought American audiences would embrace it and they didn't, so I didn't watch it for a long time. My memory is that it is a terrific picture and I don't know why. I have a theory that you shouldn't look at movies again for ten or 20 years, and watching it again recently I had the impression that it seems a splendid example of its type of movie.

'I do remember saying what the hell are we going to do about Ryan O'Neal, he's so young? But, in fact, he was the right age and it's one of those things where you are simply cursed because you have to go with it. Joe needed a star and sometimes reality just doesn't play.'

For Richard Attenborough *A Bridge Too Far* was a landmark movie. It was an international success, it had made money, and in Joe Levine it had given him the possibility of finally securing finance for his long-cherished *Gandhi*. For William Goldman it also proved to the film-making community that on his day Richard Attenborough is as good as they come. 'We can all do certain things and we can't do certain things. I can write certain things and I can't write certain things – if you want a farce, go to somebody else because I can't write one. But when he is on his game, like he was with 'Bridge' or *Gandhi*, then I think Richard Attenborough is as good as anybody.

'One of the remarkable things about Dickie is that he has managed to have a film career and stayed at home. I got into the film business in the Sixties when the studios suddenly discovered England and every major studio had an office there. That was the great height of the British film industry and then it died. The industry is so dead now that most of the top directors, the Scott brothers – Ridley and Tony – Adrian Lyne, Alan Parker, and Hugh Hudson, are now largely working in America. Dickie stayed home and had a career. He is 71 years old and is still being offered huge properties. At the end of a day we are judged by our total output and I think that the fact that he is the age he is and still doing quality work is remarkable.'

Just a part of the star-studded line-up for *A Bridge Too Far*. From left to right:
Paul Maxwell, Sean Connery, Dirk Bogarde, Edward Fox, Ryan O'Neal and
Gene Hackman

Richard Attenborough and Ben Kingsley on *Gandhi*

The funeral scene in *Gandhi*, involving the largest crowd ever assembled for a single scene in a film

A hoofer at heart? Attenborough rehearses his chorus line in *A Chorus Line*

Sound recordist Simon Kaye – an Attenborough veteran – on *Cry Freedom*

Editor Lesley Walker on location to show Attenborough her first assembly of
Cry Freedom scenes

Richard Attenborough discusses the courtroom scenes with Denzel
Washington in *Cry Freedom*

Wendy Woods helps Denzel Washington master Biko's accent between takes
on *Cry Freedom*

Kevin Kline and Richard Attenborough on *Cry Freedom*

Richard Attenborough and Donald Woods on *Cry Freedom*

Attenborough and Terry Clegg on *Cry Freedom*

A quiet moment of contemplation

Double-Cross

Filming *Magic* marked the beginning of the end of my relationship with Joe Levine. I think that those who say that if I had been able to do *Gandhi* at that point then I would not have done *Magic* are quite correct.

I think that Joe had bought the rights to Bill Goldman's novel and once again he was holding *Gandhi* over me. If I just made this one more picture for him then we would set up *Gandhi* next. He promised and promised and promised that he would do *Gandhi*, and I think it is the only time in my career I have ever been double-crossed. I sincerely believe that Joe Levine actually double-crossed me on that. He had been going to do *Gandhi* for the longest time, he kept telling me he was going to do it, and I'm not certain what it was that finally turned him against it. India came out in support of the Palestine Liberation Organisation at that time, which certainly didn't help, and he also didn't like Jackie Baroda, the Maharajah of Baroda, who was considering co-financing the film with us at the time. Nevertheless, he pulled out. But the one thing which it is important to remember about Joe was that he never put sixpence of his own money into *Gandhi*. He kept giving you the old heart-and-flowers stuff but he was playing with Paramount's money; he never put fourpence into it himself. Then when I finally went back to ask him ultimately would he or would he not do it, he said he wouldn't. I was told that I could buy it back but he didn't even negotiate with me himself, he sent me down the corridor to his accountant and his lawyer and they did the negotiating. Joe screwed me into the ground and demanded the most outrageous sum. It cost me $2 million plus 7.5 per cent of the net profits or 2.5 per cent of the gross profits to buy the film back from him. I think Joe made $4 million out of *Gandhi* for doing absolutely nothing. The irony was that he never got the one thing he most wanted as a producer, which was a Best Picture Oscar. If he had stayed with *Gandhi* then he would have got that.

Attenborough and Joe Levine in happier times

There were none of the logistical difficulties of *A Bridge Too Far* involved in shooting *Magic* but that's not to say that it wasn't without its own unique difficulties. I remember, for example, that we had the worst period of rain that anyone had ever encountered in the Catskills, where we were shooting. The long-range forecast was so bad that there was no alternative but to go ahead so we shot everything in the rain. That meant we had to change the film stock we were using but we got it done.

I think for me the attraction of *Magic* was Tony Hopkins. It was always Tony and I think really that I did the picture for him. Joe wasn't particularly fond of Tony initially. It hadn't been easy to convince Joe to cast him in *A Bridge Too Far*. Tony still wasn't that big a name at that stage, and I think Levine would have rather had someone like Sean Connery or Michael Caine or anybody, come to that, because he didn't know Tony. It was only because I once again really fought like the clappers to get him that he played Colonel Frost. But subsequently Joe became so enamoured of Tony, he thought he was simply wonderful, that he was won over by him. I think, however, Joe really financed *Magic* because he was so impressed by Bill Goldman. I think he even wanted Bill to sign a contract with him to make further pictures. But for me the combination of the two, Tony and Bill, was irresistible. I was very enamoured of them both and am still.

I think *Magic* is a better film than it is given credit for. The majority of the critics quite wrongly and without bothering even to look at it compared it to *Dead of Night*, the British movie in which Michael Redgrave plays a ventriloquist taken over by his dummy. But *Dead of Night* is a totally different story. It's quite interesting but in terms of Michael's performance and Tony's performance they are vastly dissimilar, not because Michael was not good but because it was all on one level whereas what Tony had to do was extraordinary. And being an actor I thought that the opportunity the part presented for an actor was wonderful. Ann-Margret was also cast against type to a certain extent although she had just been in *Carnal Knowledge* for Mike Nichols and I knew that she could do the job.

Over the years I have frequently found myself in situations where I have had to fight to get the cast I want, whether it was Simon Ward in *Young Winston*, Michael Douglas in *A Chorus Line* or Robert Downey Jnr in *Chaplin*. Because I'm an actor I believe, without embarrassment or false modesty, that one of the skills which I do have is that I can cast. I know how to cast good actors and I know and can feel almost intuitively the degree of skill that exists in an actor or an actress. I believe, therefore, that the casting of the movies

Richard Attenborough on the set of *Magic*

that I make is an absolutely vital element. In fact it is as important as anything that I do on the film. I have had some terrific casting directors and this is not denigrating them in any sense whatsoever, but at the end of the day they can only suggest, they can only offer up alternatives. And right down to the man who comes in and says, 'The carriage awaits', I cast my movies. I also have this instinct for knowing the potential that exists in an actor which has perhaps not been recognised to that extent up until that moment. I hardly ever test. I never make them read – they can't believe it – but I have never in my life had an actor or actress do a reading for me, I know by meeting them whether they can act or not. All the girls in *Chaplin* for instance, most of whom I had never seen act, were offered the parts on the basis of a single meeting. I just know about casting actors.

I also I think have good taste in acting. Therefore when they start to perform I know the right take to select and I know which takes work and which takes fit together. I think there are other directors who don't cast to the same extent. They don't have that same instinct and can only tell by reading or testing. In an overwhelming proportion of occasions reading actually gives you the wrong answer. I remember very clearly when I was a student in RADA in London there would frequently be an actor, a young kid, and you would say, 'God knows how they got here, they can't read to save their lives.' But the skill of actually reading a script has nothing to do with acting, it is a quite different ability. At the end of the day that particular ability is a total distraction in relation to the overall skills that are inherent if you hope to get the sort of performances that I look for. So the casting and then going through the procedure and then bringing about a judgment is what I'm best at.

When I did *Brighton Rock* I was very fortunate to have the opportunity to work with one of the best and least-heralded directors in the British film industry. His name was John Boulting. He had the most extraordinary ability with actors and what I love about directing is working with the actors. I'm not very good at the pyrotechnics of film-making, I tend to use the camera as a recorder rather than regard cinematography as an art form in its own right created by the camera and cutting. What interests me are things that I want to say and things that I care about and that I am able to say fundamentally through the actors.

I had a love scene to shoot on *Magic* between Tony and Ann-Margret. It was a very emotional scene and it was entirely necessary to the plot. But Tony, who obviously hadn't matured then into the great actor he is today, was having difficulty. He couldn't cope with the emotional intensity that was required and at one point he walked off the set. When an actor does that you have to call them back straight away. That is the only possible way you can cope with that, you have to find excuses for what an actor has done if it goes wrong. Your possibility of retrieving the situation is nil, absolutely nil, if you damage the actor's ego in front of the crew. The only time that I ever make a noise on the set is when something goes wrong with an actor either in terms of forgetting their lines or not delivering the performance as it should be and everyone knowing they're not giving the correct performance. So in those

Richard Attenborough directs Anthony Hopkins in *Magic*

situations I invariably 'lose my temper'. It's usually at David Tomblin, or Terry Clegg my executive producer, or Diana Hawkins my partner and co-producer. They know that being a scapegoat, if you like, is part of their function so that we can spare the actor's blushes. But I have also been known to lose the rag at someone who isn't even there, some mythical character. 'David,' I'll say, 'we'll have to go again, there's some bloody fool talking behind that pillar.' There's no one there, of course, but then you can turn to the actor, apologise and say, 'Can we go again, please?'

That may all be a bit of play-acting but directing does not change the fact that fundamentally I am an actor and actors like communication. They enjoy playing to an audience. Actors require an audience, it is life's blood, and they wish to convey in their communication certain thoughts and ideas. So having been in front of the camera for over 50 years, simply to chop that off because now I'm directing would not have been possible. I do work very publicly in terms of making the movies I make, I don't do it in the back room from a monitor. I work with people who very often have made several movies with me. It's a very upfront operation as far as I'm concerned so it seems to me perfectly natural that the acting persona which everything came from should be up there too.

I suppose in a way I never see a scene other than in its initial concept from any perspective except the actor's point of view and the difficulties I envisage and understand – like in that love scene in *Magic* – are all from their point of view. For instance, one thing I remember in *Gandhi* is a scene where Ben Kingsley has to make a speech in front of 20 or 30 thousand people in a valley under a canopy. His nerves were what preoccupied me more than any of the difficulties of assembling the 30,000. That's because I knew that we were in a valley and at a specific time the sun would go behind the mountain and if the sun fell below the other side of the mountain it would mean that we would be stuck, the scene would not work. It was one of the few occasions where I covered a scene with three cameras so I had the whole thing in long shot which meant that I could cut away in case Ben dried. He didn't, thank God, and he sailed straight through it. So when you are talking of a love scene and the difficulties of that scene it is really whether those two players are sufficiently relaxed and confident and sufficiently encompassed within their own belief in the scene. Whether, in fact, they are at ease with each other. The problem on *Magic* was that Tony was not really at ease with Ann-Margret, whereas in his rather more chaste bedroom scene in *Shadowlands* he was completely at ease with Debra Winger. It is interesting because there are two ways those scenes can go. There was no way of sending up the scene in *Magic*. They were much too nervous, you couldn't make jokes about Tony being in bed with Ann-Margret because she was so conscious of her sexual profile, her reputation as America's favourite cheerleader, as it were. So you couldn't send it up, but these two characters on *Shadowlands* were constantly teasing each other and so that feeling of relaxation flowed over them. And I think at the end of the day the results are there to see on the screen. There would have been no question of Tony leaving the set on *Shadowlands*.

'Peggy Ann Snow, Peggy Ann Snow . . .'

The seeds that would grow into *Magic* were sown in unlikely surroundings. The psychological chiller about a psychotic ventriloquist had its origins at a lavish Hollywood-style birthday party for disco king Allan Carr. Carr was the man behind movies like *Grease* and *Can't Stop the Music*. He also went on to produce one of the most heavily criticised Oscar-night shows in living memory. However, for his birthday he had assembled a company for dinner at Regine's nightspot in Paris which included actress Ann-Margret and her husband, Roger Smith, along with William Goldman and his wife. Goldman and the versatile entertainer got talking and over dinner they discovered that not only were they both from Illinois, they had also gone to high school there, and rival high schools at that.

'While we were talking about our schooldays I mentioned that I had been a cheerleader,' recalls Ann-Margret. 'Then when William started writing *Magic* he told me afterwards that he had written it with me in mind. My name in the movie is Peggy Ann Snow and since Peggy is short for Margaret her real name is Margaret Ann. My stage name is Ann-Margret so he wrote it with me in mind and I was absolutely thrilled.'

In *Magic* Anthony Hopkins plays Corky, a young magician who has studied for years at the feet of a once-legendary stage performer now seeking solace through drink. Corky takes the stage to make his début at an amateur night and dies on his feet. He drops out of sight for a few years and sharpens the act by introducing Fats, a wise-cracking, foul-mouthed, heckling ventriloquist's dummy. The results are sensational and he becomes an overnight success even though he insists on still playing the same theatre where he bombed first time out. Carefully managed by veteran agent Burgess Meredith, Corky is destined for the big time. The only thing standing between him and success is a routine medical which is required by the TV network before they will commit to the variety special which will launch him coast to coast. Corky fears that the medical will reveal the creeping psychosis which he is beginning to suspect he is developing so he gets out of town fast.

With no real place to go Corky seeks refuge in his past. On his way to the legendary Grossinger's Resort in the Catskills he stops off at a small, run-down holiday complex. The place is being run by Peg, the cheerleader on whom Corky had a crush in high school. He books a chalet without revealing who he is. She recognises him straight away and once they overcome their initial reserve they begin an affair. There are problems, however, in the shape of her boorish husband, played by Ed Lauter, and Corky's growing mental problems. As the voice of his subconscious, Fats exerts a greater and greater influence as Corky descends further and further into the depths of paranoid schizophrenia. It is a descent which will lead to murder and threaten the life of the one person Corky cherishes above all others.

William Goldman is very fond of *Magic*, not just his own novel but the movie Richard Attenborough crafted from his script. 'He assembled a wonderful cast of actors and it looked just as I had imagined it,' he says. 'Especially Peggy. If you're in America then cheerleaders are a special part of your life and in my head I had always imagined Peggy as a cheerleader. Ann-Margret is everybody's dream and I thought she was just wonderful. I thought Tony Hopkins was great too. I like the movie.'

But for all his fondness for the finished work and his admiration for Attenborough as a director, Goldman still hasn't quite fathomed why he did it. *Magic* and *A Chorus Line* are two films which, for him, are aberrations in the director's career. *Magic*, however, meant that Attenborough was once again working for Joe Levine, producer of *A Bridge Too Far*, even if that wasn't the way it was initially supposed to be.

'Dickie was not the original director for *Magic*,' Goldman recalls. 'The original script was done for Norman Jewison. I'm not privy to what happened next but Jewison and Levine had an argument and I don't know what it was about. I don't know whether Joe provoked the argument because Dickie was unavailable or not but I do know that Levine was crazy about Attenborough at this point. Dickie took very good care of Joe, he knew how to stroke his ego. Levine could be very cranky but he liked being around Dickie because he would basically make him feel involved in the process. But, whatever the reason, the first two drafts had been for Jewison and Attenborough came on late. I was thrilled, however, because I had enjoyed working with him so much on *A Bridge Too Far*.

Whether it was to stay alive, whether it was to pay bills, or whether it was in the hope that Levine would ultimately make good on his promises about *Gandhi*, Goldman is still mystified by Attenborough's decision to make the film. After three large-scale war movies the prospect of a story which was effectively a two-hander may have seemed an odd choice.

'I don't mean this as crassly as it probably sounds,' says Goldman qualifying his curiosity. 'What I mean is that if you're a director you want to work and Dickie's passion was *Gandhi*. He would talk about *Gandhi* during our discussions on "Bridge". He did a fine job with my story but I don't know why he did *Magic* because it has none of that liberal admiration at play that Dickie needs when he is inflamed and when he is at his best. Neither did *A Chorus Line*; there are no causes in either movie and in almost all of his work that is the thing which drives his motor. I believe that he had a good time on "Bridge" and I think he thought he could make a good film out of *Magic* – which he did. But my guess is that if he had been able to get *Gandhi* off the ground at that time then he wouldn't have made *Magic*.'

Attenborough's choice for a male lead was Anthony Hopkins. It was he who, as Corky, slipped into the abyss of madness crooning all the while. 'Peggy Ann Snow, Peggy Ann Snow, please let me follow wherever you go.' In spite of roles opposite Goldie Hawn in *The Girl from Petrovka* and Marsha Mason in *Audrey Rose*, Hopkins still hadn't broken through to American audiences. That wouldn't come until *The Silence of the Lambs*, which was still some 13 years away. However, he had worked twice before with Attenborough. In *Young Winston* he played a cameo as his fellow Welshman, the politician David Lloyd George, and he appeared to great effect as the charismatic Colonel Frost in *A Bridge Too Far*. Like Goldman, he was well aware that getting *Gandhi* off the ground was a consuming passion for his director.

'About a year after I had played Lloyd George for him we went out to lunch,' explains Hopkins. 'Dickie said to me: "Right, I want you to play Gandhi." So I looked over my shoulder to see who he was talking to and realised it was me. "You want me to play Gandhi?" I asked. "No one else can play it," he told me. "You'll be wonderful." I thought he was joking but it went on for a few years like that. As a consequence when I was doing *A Bridge Too Far* he was still trying to get Joe Levine to do *Gandhi*. And I think he also did *Magic* on the strength of it and he was still keen while we were shooting it. I think, though, it was a bit of a brainstorm on his part and silly vanity on mine to think that I could do it. I never actually got so far as testing for the part but I did run up and down the sides of mountains and ate bean shoots to lose weight. Every time I looked in the mirror I still looked like someone who should be in the front row of a rugby scrum. So eventually I phoned him one day and we both sort of agreed that we had no chance.'

Like Richard Attenborough, writer William Goldman is also annoyed at the most consistent criticism levelled at *Magic*, namely that it was a rip-off from *Dead of Night* the 1946 British horror anthology. 'That's one of those asshole critic things,' he says, still aggrieved and he believes justifiably. '*Dead of Night* suffered from being compared to the von Stroheim movie *The Great Gabbo*. The story in *Dead of Night* was 14 minutes in an anthology movie. *Magic* was based on a novel of mine which had been bought by Levine and I had turned into a screenplay. I love *Dead of Night* but I certainly didn't say: "Oh boy, let's rip off this story because it was such a fabulously successful 14 minutes that everybody talks about."

'I don't know whether *Magic* was a little ahead of its time or not. The movie was successful and money was made. It was not a huge hit but it was a commercial success in America and I thought Tony and Ann-Margret were great.

'I think, though, it was always at its best in post-production. There's a thing that directors do where they put what they call a "temp score" on to their movies while they're in post-production, and generally they take music from other similar films and lay down a temporary soundtrack. Dickie apparently had a terrifying temp score with music from Bernard Herrmann's great score for *Psycho*. The movie was apparently at its most terrifying then. Then they put in the real score, which was fine, but it went for a more romantic tone than the Herrmann music and it was not as scary.'

One of the toughest scenes emotionally in *Magic* is the 'pick-a-card' sequence between Corky and Peg. They've been out for a romantic walk by the lake and she has been quizzing him about his magic. He insists it doesn't exist, it's just a trick. 'Magic is misdirection,' he tells her. However, she teases him and goads him into doing a trick. Back in the cabin Corky settles down to show her a simple mind-reading stunt designed to demonstrate the glamorous assistant's love for the magician. She has to pick a card and hold it next to her heart. If she loves him enough then he will be able to pick up her thoughts and tell her what the card is.

Through a series of cross-cuts and distorted camera angles Attenborough manages to imbue this ordinary scene with hidden menace. This is the moment when Corky finally goes over the edge and Peggy ends up in genuine fear of the consequences if he guesses wrong. The trick turns out alright but instead of proving how much she loves him it has instead shown her a side of Corky which will haunt her for the rest of the picture.

It's a tough scene which puts demands on the actress playing Peggy. Although she had done *Carnal Knowledge* for Mike Nichols and ironically, considering Levine's original intentions, *The Cincinatti Kid* for Norman Jewison, Ann-Margret had never played a role like Peggy Ann Snow. Attenborough bravely cast her against type. Movie audiences knew her as the flame-haired dynamo gyrating with Elvis Presley in *Viva Las Vegas* but Attenborough wanted them to accept her as a faded beauty who has grown old before her time through choosing the wrong man. The director and his star both knew it would require a lot of work to get the sort of performance they both wanted.

'Richard took such a lot of time with me,' says Ann-Margret. 'I am a totally emotional, instinctive actress. I'm not technical – I can't cry to camera four when you want me to – I'm not a robot. But he knew exactly what to tell me. He never ever raised his voice because if anyone shouts at me I just crumble, I'm gone. There was never any yelling in my house when I grew up and I can't handle anyone like that.

'Filming *Magic* turned into a wonderful experience for me. He was so gentle and he always found the right things to say. Even during the love scene which Tony and I had to do, he was always supportive. He always said the right thing at the right time and I appreciated that a great deal.'

Both Attenborough and Ann-Margret were rewarded for their efforts. *Magic* was a solid commercial success and she and Hopkins both drew rave

Attenborough discusses a scene from *Magic* with Ann-Margret

reviews for their performances. There were no rave reviews for the other cast member, the inanimate one, although perhaps there ought to have been. 'Fats' the dummy was an omnipresent malevolent force in the picture. Attenborough kept him constantly at the edge of Corky's psychosis and the audience's attention. Ann-Margret doesn't enjoy watching her own movies; watching *Magic* would have been a particular ordeal since she doesn't like scary movies because they give her nightmares. *Magic*, she says, was one of the scariest films she had ever seen.

'What really scared me was that they had three different dummies to be used as the story developed in the course of the movie,' she explains with the relative security of 15 years' hindsight. 'The first one was cherubic, with a cherubic little face. The second one had a kind of strangeness about it you couldn't put your finger on, and the third one was downright scary. I was always worried because I never knew quite where they were going to be. I remember one occasion when I was going back to my dressing-room after a take and I happened to turn round and about an inch away from me was this grotesque third dummy. I jumped about ten feet in the air. Everyone laughed but I was really scared because they seemed so real.'

For his part, looking back on the film Fats's human partner, Anthony Hopkins, says, although he enjoyed the experience very much, he was aware of

Richard Attenborough and 'Fats' share a quiet moment in *Magic*

feeling out of his depth. He found himself, he recalls, in something of a dilemma.

'I was very pleased to have been given the chance to do it, but I was also very conscious that an American actor should have been playing the part. I thought I had been pretty foolish to accept it in the first place. I was very scared of the accent and all that. You have to understand that this was 15 years ago and I've changed a lot in those 15 years. I've matured a lot as an actor but in those days I tended to eat the scenery. But I ended up being able to cope because Dickie went out of his way to make me feel at ease.

'For example, to help me prepare for the "pick-a-card" scene he brought a magician over to my flat. The magician, who was actually a bank manager, gave me a pack of cards to see if I could handle them. At my first attempt they went all over the floor, leaving Dickie in tears of maniacal laughter. So this bank manager told me that if I was going to look convincing I would have to have a pack of cards in my hand at all times. He showed me how to do a one-hand shuffle, how to roll a coin over my knuckles, and all that kind of stuff. I have to say I was a good student and I picked up the basics very quickly.'

So, armed with enough knowledge of conjuring to get steady work on the

76

children's party circuit, Hopkins went to Hollywood to film *Magic*. But as the filming progressed and the time came to shoot the mind-reading sequence he began to feel more and more unhappy.

'I was disappointed,' he admits with hindsight. 'I didn't feel it was working but Dickie would say it was fine. He printed the scene and we broke for lunch. I was sitting having a nice lunch in my trailer when he came in and said: "Are you alright?" "No I'm not," I told him, "I just don't feel like I'm doing anything, I don't feel like I'm working." But he said: "Don't worry, you don't have to do all that stuff, we'll get the magician to do all the close-up stuff." But I persisted. "I can do some of that," I said. "I know," he replied, "but you can't do all of it because you're not a magician. You're not a ventriloquist either. What do you want to do?" he asked. "You can't do everything. Just keep doing the best you can, the crew happens to think you're doing a wonderful job!"

'So he was always very reassuring because he is such a superb craftsman himself and that is a great help to an actor.'

Like Simon Ward before him and Ben Kingsley and Robert Downey Jnr after him, Anthony Hopkins was not a major movie name when he found himself carrying a Richard Attenborough picture. Attenborough thrives on discovering new talent, he loves casting movies almost as much as directing them, but he is not overly protective of his discoveries.

'There's no cotton wool or anything like that,' laughs Hopkins. 'Sometimes he gets a bit ratty because some producer or studio executive has been a bit of a pain and he'll snarl a bit and laugh that wild laugh. But he'll keep all of that away from you, none of that pressure comes down on you. What he does is he delegates, because if you're directing a film and you try to do everyone's job you'll go mad. Some directors do want to do everything. They want to act for you, they want to do the make-up, they want to do everything. They're pure and simple control freaks. They may be very nice men but they're hell on earth to work with. These guys want to be everywhere but Dickie doesn't. He appreciates people. He doesn't interfere and he doesn't mess about.

'He won't pretend to be an expert either, which is also important. He may not be a musician but he might ask whoever is scoring his picture: "Can you give me a bit more of this or a touch less of that?" When you can go to an expert and ask if they can help you out then that to me is the mark of real professional humility.

'I think he is the best director I have ever worked with as well as the most generous friend. What he has done professionally for this country and so many people is priceless, he is a great, great man.'

Gandhiji

My interest in *Gandhi* began in 1962 when I got a call from Motilal Kothari, a civil servant working at the Indian High Commission in London, to ask if I would consider making a film about Mahatma Gandhi. Over lunch we talked about the Mahatma and he asked if I would read Louis Fischer's biography and then let him know whether I was still interested. I was shortly to go on holiday with my wife, Sheila, and my then partner, Bryan Forbes, and his actress wife, Nanette Newman, so I said I would read the book while I was away.

I remember lying on the bed and starting to read this huge volume. Early in the book there was an incident recalled which just gave me goose pimples. It was an account of a moment when Gandhiji was walking down the street in South Africa with another Indian and towards him came two white South Africans and, as was expected of them, Gandhiji and his friend stepped into the gutter to let the whites pass on the pavement. After they had gone by Gandhiji said to his colleague, without any anger or resentment, 'You know, it is always a mystery to me why men should feel themselves honoured by the humiliation of their fellow human beings.' I was absolutely bowled over when I read that. Particularly because the young man was 19 at the time. I thought this was one of the most extraordinarily perceptive observations in terms of human relations that I had ever read. It was probably that one incident which set me on the road to making this film, a road which would take 18 years to reach its final destination.

I have to pay tribute to the patience and support of my wife during those 18 years. Sheila is incredibly understanding, especially of the risks that were taken financially and in security terms in my trying to make a film about Gandhi. She never tried to talk me out of it – even when we got to the point where we could scarcely pay the gas bill. Never once did she say, 'You

Richard Attenborough and Motilal Kothari discuss an early *Gandhi* script with Indira Gandhi in Delhi in September 1964

shouldn't be taking these risks', or 'We should come first.' She absolutely understood my sense of commitment and that has applied to everything I have ever done.

Aside from actually raising the money to make the film, the problems with *Gandhi* were largely logistical. The great difficulty with sequences of massively complicated logistics is that you can be so wrongly seduced into thinking that they work well just because they work at all. It's easy to think that because they did all come over the hill at the right moment that's all that matters, but the manner in which they came over the hill is also very important. In *A Bridge Too Far* we had similar problems with the advance of the tanks and the scene where the tanks are coming into the square. It's very hard and thank God after the third or fourth take it did work. They all came into the square and they came into the square the way they were supposed to. People always say, 'How did you manage that?' but the load of

Opposite: Richard Attenborough with Ben Kingsley as Gandhi. This is Attenborough's favourite photograph from the film

responsibility is as much on the actors as it is on the director or the producer. If you have assembled 30,000 people and the sun is going down over the mountain and Ben Kingsley has to deliver a perforation of some kind and he buggers it up, poor devil, then he knows perfectly well what he's done. He can see just as well as I can that the sun is going down; therefore the pressures on him are no less than those on the producer or director.

It was very frightening when we went from talking about making *Gandhi* to actually making *Gandhi*. Everything I had done up until then had been a rehearsal of sorts but thank God in a way I didn't succeed immediately. I began trying in 1962 to set it up and of course it wasn't until 1969 that I started to direct and it was 1980 when we actually shot. It was a miracle really that I was forced into those other experiences. Whatever success or lack of it *Oh! What A Lovely War* may have had there is no question whatsoever that it was the kind of movie which was domestic, relatively cheap, relatively under control, and shot in the best summer that anyone ever remembers in the history of the UK. It was unbelievable we had only one sequence where it rained – the French sequence where we had to sit around on top of the Sussex Downs for a few days. The point that I'm making is that experiment and innovation was applicable and indeed appropriate to *Oh! What A Lovely War*. When you start up something of the scale of *Gandhi* you really can't make a mistake and never could that be better exemplified than in the funeral sequence. We had to know exactly what we were about. If we weren't sufficiently prepared, if we weren't quite certain as to the impact that we wanted, or indeed sufficiently conscious of what lenses would do and what angles would mean – all of which, or a vast part of which, was unknown to me in 1969 – the funeral scene and the picture itself would simply not have worked.

Once again I owe an enormous debt to David Tomblin, who was the first assistant on *Gandhi*, for his skill and planning. Nothing happens by chance when David is around. We had, for instance, a crowd of 400,000 people for Gandhi's funeral – which, incidentally, put us in the *Guinness Book of Records* for having the largest crowd ever seen on screen. I think we employed 150,000 and we anticipated another 100,000 turning up on the day and in fact we got an additional 250,000. But David was ready. He anticipated and we had rehearsed that scene until the principals screamed with boredom. We had rehearsed the cortège procession on a disused aerodrome mapped out yard by yard. We had to teach the troops the slow march, which they had abandoned since Independence, and David was in the Marines so he was just the man to do it. Weekend after weekend we rehearsed this. In addition, we had to be absolutely certain that whatever drama occurred, whatever went wrong, the fundamental shape and form of filming it was set. Eleven camera positions were employed, the cameras were all shooting different aspects and you couldn't stop it once the thing started. There were 250,000 people there who had come to pay tribute to Gandhiji: they weren't extras, they were there to pay tribute. David had them all in various sections and you had to go through a gate to get to each particular

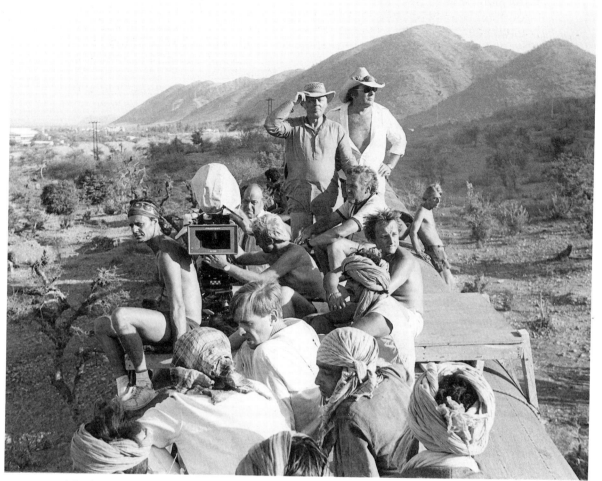

The last day of Indian location shooting on *Gandhi*. David Tomblin is standing behind Attenborough

section. At each gate there was someone who would buy the modern clothes off them and exchange them for costumes so that they looked right. We had gone so far as to make sure these people on the gate were armed with fistfuls of cash for that purpose – every wrong piece of clothing was bought so that they all looked broadly the appropriate colour.

David would have all this worked out like a regimental sergeant major, he knew exactly what was happening. We would go up every Saturday and work it all out. We would put Mountbatten here, Nehru there, and Patel somewhere else. But without that commitment it simply wouldn't have happened. David has a thing the Americans have which we don't have. David has a pride in what he does, knowing that he is as good as anybody doing the job and his satisfaction is in doing that job, not yearning for something else.

As of that moment, that was satisfactory for him and he knew exactly what he required. He commanded that procession like a general. He was there with his microphone and all of his assistants were on walkie-talkies. He had them all in the crowd dressed as extras so he could stay in communication with them – he could move 10,000 people to the left with a single command, it was extraordinary. I even dressed up and got in the shot myself because it was the only way I could direct the whole thing. In the actual finished film there is a shot of me walking backwards behind the cortège with the hair down on my shoulders and nobody has ever spotted it. If you look at the sideways shot of the cortège with the figure lying on the bier, right behind the figure is me dressed as a brigadier or whatever it is, but I'm actually walking backwards directing people unashamedly in the shot.

No matter what else I had done up until then, *Gandhi* was always in my mind in exactly the same way that my ambition to make a movie about the revolutionary Thomas Paine is now and has been for Lord knows how long. But it wasn't just the experience of big movies like *A Bridge Too Far* which stood me in good stead with *Gandhi*. I think that my time on *Young Winston* with Simon – who was equivalent in a way to Ben, in that he was carrying a movie never having done film, in the same way that Ben had never done film – was immensely useful. I think that a certain number of the problems which were self-evident with Simon, also had to be dealt with in some form or another when they arose with Ben. Although he was a more experienced theatre player he was just as ignorant as far as film was concerned.

Casting *Gandhi* had always been a problem. Over the years we had considered actors like Peter Finch, Dirk Bogarde, Tony Hopkins and Albert Finney. At one point an American studio told me if I could cast Richard Burton I could have the money. Pandit Nehru in fact wanted Alec Guinness to play it. Nehru was the most sage of characters with a wonderful sophistication coupled with a complete lack of stupid and destructive chauvinism. He said simply that the film about Gandhi would probably only be made once as a biography, that *Nine Hours to Rama* – the Hollywood version of his assassination – had been an outrage in his opinion, and that the importance of the film was to introduce Gandhi to the rest of the world. Yes, of course it was relevant to the new generations in India but there were many, many millions of people outside India who really knew damn all about him. If this was to happen and if this was to work then some compromises would have to be made. To think that the film could work with the style of acting and the concept of performance which was absolutely acceptable and indeed demanded in India was unrealistic. That style was totally unacceptable in the rest of the world and Nehru believed that if it was going to be convincing somehow or another it had to have the reality that Western performances and Western characterisations were abounding in.

In Nehru's opinion Alec Guinness was capable of playing anything. That was in 1962 and it may be that in 1962 if Alec had said yes it may just have been possible that the conventions of cinema in that time would have allowed a European to put dark stain on his skin, just as Anthony Quinn had done in

Opposite: Brigadier Attenborough synchronises his watch on *Gandhi*

Lawrence of Arabia, and get away with it. Alec actually said no because he felt that it was not within his range, but he also disapproved of a European playing the part. Twenty years later, however, the conventions had changed and you could not simply take a European actor and make him up to look like an Indian. Therefore, although I had talked to that long list of people at varying times during the 20 years, the more I thought about it, and the more concerned I was about the casting, the more certain I became that it had to be in some form an Indian. Indeed, I had meetings with the only director in India at that time who had any pretensions of a Western style of performance, and that was Satyajit Ray. He, in large measure, actually echoed my own feelings but was extremely reticent and doubtful about the possibility of finding an Indian actor of the scope that the role entailed. One of the things that Nehru had said was that you could get an Indian actor who he was sure could be taught to do a relatively small segment, but to have an actor to carry the movie you really had to have somebody of theatrical experience of some sort.

I was somewhat at my wits' end by this stage. It was, in fact, my son Michael who said one day, 'Dad, did you ever see Peter Brook's "Dream?"', I said I had and he said, 'Don't you remember an actor called Ben Kingsley?' Everyone knows how rotten I am at names but it still didn't really mean anything to me as such. Then I got some pictures and Michael had said, 'Apart from anything else he's half Indian.' I said, 'You're joking.' But he wasn't. Ben's real name is Krishna Banjhi, and Michael had assumed I must have known about his background. We went to see him in *Baal*, which was almost a one-man show, and then when he was in *Nicholas Nickleby* I rang him at the Aldwych stage door and asked if I could come to see him. He thought it was a gag when somebody said: 'Dickie Attenborough is on the phone for you.' After we had spoken he went to check with Trevor Nunn and he certainly didn't believe that I actually wanted to talk to him seriously. What Trevor said to Ben was: 'Of course you must do it, it's the part you were born for.' We then decided, after a great deal of to-ing and fro-ing that there really were only two possible actors that we should test and they were John Hurt and Ben. John did the first test and said, 'Dick I have seen Ben Kingsley getting made-up and dressed and I look like a rugby full-back from Yorkshire. I look idiotic, I look ludicrous, and I can't manage the clothes. I can't do anything. This man is a wonderful actor, everybody admires him, he will be phenomenal.' And of course what happened was that – good as John Hurt's performance was as a performance – he was dead right in his assessment. When Ben walked on the floor it was like Robert Downey years later in *Chaplin*, you just knew that he was the man to do it, it was absolutely within his capability. John came down the next day and decided not even to watch the tests, he couldn't bear it, bless him. He said: 'Let's call it a day right here and now, I'm sure you've got a wonderful performance from Kingsley haven't you?' 'Yes,' I said, 'You were right John, he is absolutely incredible.'

I hadn't seen *Gandhi* for some time but I watched it recently at a special screening at the Winter Garden, an old variety theatre on the island of Bute off the West Coast of Scotland where Sheila and I have a home. Looking back, for me the attraction was always working with Ben. He was extraordinary, he was remarkable, but so were others. Ian Charleson, in particular. His performance in the scene in the prison cell when Ben tells him he must go away and he must leave the Indians to plough their own furrow, to make their own case, to promulgate their own views and that others mustn't do it for them, is quite remarkable. Seeing these two deeply close friends separating on this principle is acting at its absolute top. Also Rohini Hattangady's performance as Gandhi's wife is also quite extraordinary. She did one scene in the prison where she plays the old woman in which she was wonderful. The point is that as I recall the movie now it isn't, 'Wow what a shot that was', or 'Wow look at the scale of this sequence.' It is indicative that what I recall and witness again with such joy is a performance and that's what's fascinating.

Gandhi of course was a huge commercial success and much of that had to do with its showing at the Academy Awards. I have to say in all truth that our surprise at winning awards was first encountered not at the Oscars but at the Directors Guild awards dinner. The Directors Guild, with I think only three or four exceptions, usually indicates the winner of the Best Director Oscar. What I said at the time, and this is absolutely genuine and people still don't believe it because they say I'm being falsely modest and I'm not, is that Steven Spielberg should have won. We went to the Directors Guild dinner absolutely convinced in our own minds that *ET* and Steven Spielberg would win it. Indeed he would not only win it but in my opinion and my judgment – and again people will say, 'Rubbish he doesn't mean it' – we genuinely believed he ought to have won it. I thought *ET* was the more exciting, wonderful, innovative piece of film, as against *Gandhi* which fitted into the David Lean mould in terms not of cinematic execution but of concept and sweep. So we knew in our hearts that this was going to be very exciting, we would probably never ever go to the Directors Guild again so we should certainly go and it would be wonderful just to be there. The podium was in the middle and Steven and I were at opposite sides of the room, and when the winner's name was announced after all the speeches and such I literally had to be nudged. I couldn't believe it. I got up from the table and it was a sort of knee-jerk actor's reaction. I didn't go to the podium, I went over to Spielberg. He got up, I put my arms round him and I said, 'This isn't right, this should be yours', and then I went to collect the award. Steven sweetly tells that story when people ask him. 'No, I've never won an Oscar,' he would say, although this was before *Schindler's List*, 'but I have what I consider to be an honorary Oscar, because when Dickie was announced as the winner of the Directors Guild award instead of going up to collect it he came over and said, "This should be yours."' I have to say that I meant what I told him, I absolutely genuinely meant that.

By virtue of the fact that historically Oscars go to Directors Guild winners I had to assume that there was a chance that *Gandhi* might now pull it off on Oscar night. Equally, I think we all felt that the pendulum might swing the

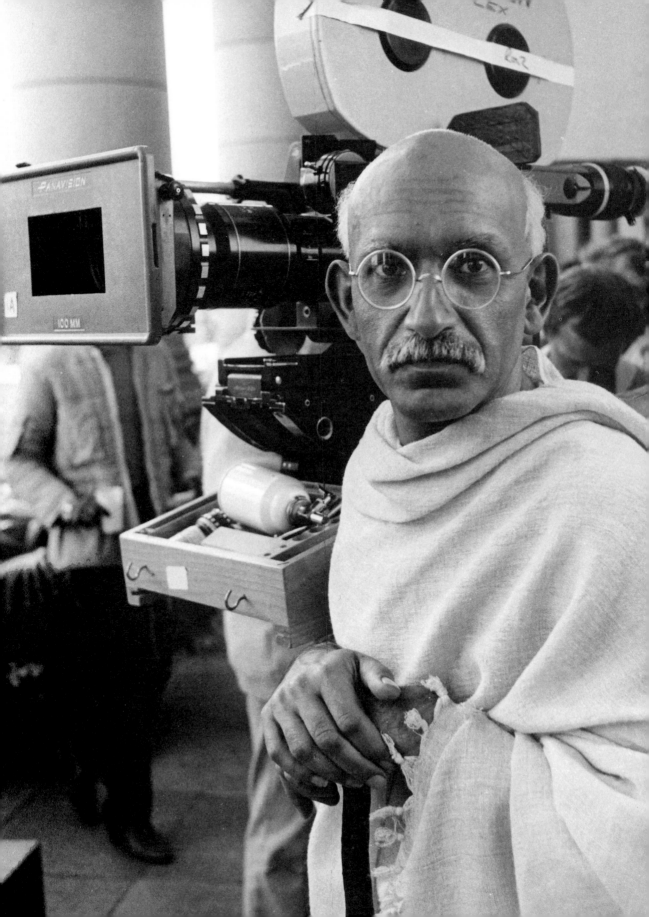

other way because it has happened in the past. People might say of the Directors Guild: 'That's one of the most ridiculous decisions anyone has ever made – we will all rally behind *ET.*' So we went to the Oscars knowing that there was a possibility but we were really very ambivalent. We didn't go thinking it was ours by any means, we were looking for all sorts of signs and portents. If you're going to win and you start getting the minor awards you almost know for sure that it's a sweep. The first sign was when Bhanu Aithaya and John Mollo won for Best Costumes – and the costumes in *Gandhi* were good but they were not super special – we then started to pull in the other awards. As we got through right to Ben, which we did think was a hell of a chance because it was a bewildering performance, we then began to think that we might make it. Then when we got Best Director our hearts really were absolutely pumping because there was a chance we would get Best Picture which, of course, is what we did. That win revolutionised and profoundly affected our ultimate receipts and established us as the largest number of Oscars ever won by a British picture. It was absolutely staggering.

The perpetual question is always: 'What do you think of the Oscars? What do they mean to you? Are they a load of old rubbish? Do you despise them?' My answer is always: 'Absolutely not.' I do not despise them, I do not have my Oscars holding the loo door open or anything like that, they go up on the mantelpiece in my office and I'm very proud to have got them. Whether you think they are commercialised or whether you think they are obtained by the pressure brought about by advertising campaigns, the fact is they are dead straight. They are absolutely on the level, nobody knows other than the official auditors Price Waterhouse until that evening. Nobody knows and they are not rigged and 5,000 people, who are your peers, vote for them. You may approve or not approve of the process, you may think the decisions are wise or ill-judged, but the fact is that when you do win you have won it by virtue of their judgment. The other question, about the value of an Oscar, is answered by the fact that our batch of Oscars made a tremendous difference to our ultimate take. We went to a cinema one afternoon to check the print of *Gandhi.* There had been a lunchtime screening and there had been two men and a dog in the cinema and I think the dog was the only one who was awake. To say that they were beating the doors down would have been something of an exaggeration; by about five in the afternoon the nominations were announced in Los Angeles and there was a queue at the box office in Stockholm. Nobody thought the film would do business, they thought it would be okay but for there to be a queue to get into the theatre for the evening performance could only be simply because that afternoon the nominations had been announced. So anyone who suggests that anyone who makes movies doesn't care about the Oscars, that they think it is somehow beneath them artistically, is talking rubbish. If they make movies that they care about and they want to go on making movies that they care about, then financial viability is a prerequisite for the future. The Oscar can do that and that's why it is important.

Opposite: Ben Kingsley as Gandhiji

Richard Attenborough directs Edward Fox as General Dyer in a tense scene from *Gandhi*

Climbing the Mountain

It was close to Christmas in 1962 when Richard Attenborough got the phone call which first interested him in doing a screen biography of Mahatma Gandhi. It was close to Christmas 18 years later when the cameras actually rolled and filming finally began. From that phone call from Indian civil servant Motilal Kothari to the moment when the first foot of film was actually shot, there had been 18 years of heartbreak, disappointment, and frustration as Attenborough's cherished project was snatched away again and again. One of the biggest disappointments was that 'Moti', who had come to be a close and loyal friend, had died before the film was finished and so never saw what he had set in train so many years before. Attenborough had never consciously intended to become a director, he had only wanted to direct *Gandhi*. His four films before this had been, in truth, an elongated dress rehearsal for one of the passions of his life.

So on the morning of 26 November 1980 at the Batra stone works some 25 miles west of Delhi the film was finally about to begin. The first scene to be shot was one of the young Mohandas K. Gandhi leading one of his early protests outside a South African mine. Everything was set. The cast was there with Ben Kingsley about to begin the role which would win him an Oscar, the crew was there with the redoubtable David Tomblin dragooning them into formation, even the giant Louma crane which allows 360-degree pans was there. Only one thing was missing; the director. After 18 years of fighting and battling to get the picture made, Richard Attenborough was late for the first day of filming. A man who lives by the clock was not on the floor at the appointed time.

Attenborough's apparent tardiness is the one thing vividly etched in the memory of Terry Clegg, the man responsible for overseeing this massive production. But as he looks back on it, the explanation for the director's

Attenborough discusses a scene with Ian Charleson who played Charlie Andrews in *Gandhi*

absence was as typical as his lateness was atypical. 'The first day was obviously a great landmark for all of us,' says Clegg. 'We had actually got there and we had this huge outfit ready to roll. We were due to shoot part of the South African mine sequence where the miners are having a demonstration against the mine owners. It was a hefty day, in fact a tough day to be starting a shoot because we had crowds and action and horses. And Dickie turned up late. I didn't know why and I didn't ask at the time, but later in the morning I asked one of his assistants what had been the problem. He told me, "He went to see the Mahatma." Dickie had gone on his own to the place where Gandhi was cremated and spent 45 minutes there. He left everyone else and walked round and sat there obviously communing with the old chap, saying what he had to say and obviously asking for a little bit of help. It made him the best part of an hour late but it wasn't a problem because he knew very well we had things that we had to do. We just couldn't believe that here was the director late on set after almost 20 years waiting.'

Terry Clegg describes the financing of *Gandhi* as traumatic, which demonstrates his flair for understatement. Richard Attenborough gives his absorbing version of the story in his own book *In Search of Gandhi*. The film had been shopped round every studio in Hollywood, every British company had been offered the chance, Attenborough himself had mortgaged his house and borrowed against his art collection. It wasn't until Goldcrest got involved in July 1980 that the film finally looked like getting a green light. The original deal for the $19 million film was for 20th Century Fox to put up about half – surprising since it was a Fox executive who uttered the immortal quote: 'Who the hell do you think is interested in making a movie about a little brown man dressed in a sheet and carrying a beanpole.' The Indian government was investing several million through its National Film Development Corporation, and the remaining $4 million was being provided by Goldcrest and other investors. There was a major blow when Fox pulled out but they were quickly replaced in part by an Indian family who promised $4 million of private funds. That left Goldcrest boss Jake Eberts to find the rest, which he thought he had secured with a complicated leasing deal through Barclays Bank. Catastrophically, Barclays said they couldn't go through with the arrangement but by the time they made up their mind shooting had already begun. The financing of *Gandhi* was always going to be fraught but for Terry Clegg and especially Richard Attenborough this was a time of enormous frustration.

'I think it had been traumatic up to the point where we started shooting because I think in his heart Dickie didn't really believe it was going to happen,' says Clegg. 'After 20 years of pushing and pulling every string he could think of, he hoped that it was going to be there. But he'd been so close so many times before I think that even when we got close he was convinced the bottom was going to fall out of it. There was a period, in fact about a week before shooting started, when a large portion of the Indian money still wasn't in place. I said to him: "We'll have to think seriously about this because if we go that extra yard now we will be heavily committed and there is no way back. Is this what you want to do?" At that stage I knew he was very heavily committed personally but I wasn't entirely aware of how deeply he had committed himself. But he is a very determined man and that is one of his great assets. He sets goals and when he steers towards that goal nothing is going to deflect him.'

Shooting began with the belief that the Barclays deal was in place. When they pulled out in December Eberts made frantic efforts to find a replacement but without success. In the end, as he details in his book *My Indecision is Final*, he went back to the board of Goldcrest and asked them to come up with the money. He also promised that this was absolutely the last money that they would have to put up for the film. Happily, because of Terry Clegg's good husbandry, the film was on schedule and keeping to its budget and Ebert's guarantee would probably have been correct. However, in February 1981 the family providing the private Indian finance pulled out. Eberts was devastated. Filming was so far advanced it would have been foolish to stop but without the $4 million in place they would then default on payments in India and the film

James Callaghan visits the *Gandhi* set in Poona. Attenborough is the gracious host, though he knew the picture was in danger of being abandoned

would have to be wound up. Eberts went to James Lee of Pearson Longman, the merchant bank which was Goldcrest's principal shareholder. Both men knew the severity of the situation but before he would guarantee the money Lee flew out to India for a crisis meeting with Terry Clegg and Attenborough.

Clegg and Lee met for dinner in a hotel in Poona at which Lee was adamant he had to have assurances that this $4 million would be the absolute amount needed to finish the film. While this crisis meeting was taking place Attenborough, who was also completely aware of the gravity of the situation, was in the same hotel entertaining former British Prime Minister James Callaghan with their respective wives.

'I felt confident,' Clegg recalls. 'I had done my sums and at that point in the movie when we were two thirds through the location I felt that I knew what it would take to complete it. Callaghan had Jack Cunningham, his parliamentary private secretary, with him at the time and I know Jack was enormously amused by Dickie's stories. He was doing impressions of Noel Coward and telling stories about John Mills and Gielgud; he loves all this stuff.

He's an actor through and through and I could see all this happening from about 12 feet away where I was sitting with James Lee giving him my heart and soul about what we needed to finish the movie. I also knew at this point that the bank account was almost dry. If James and Pearson Longman had not finally agreed to come to the rescue when they did then without question the movie would have had to be shut down.

'That doesn't mean to say we would have abandoned it because then we would have had to have gone the traditional Hollywood route of taking parts of the film round the studios and showing them some cut material to drum up the money through a distribution deal. All of that would have affected our final distribution agreement and would have made all the difference to those of us who had been given a share in it – as is Dickie's custom – as to whether or not it was going to be profitable. A delay at this stage would have had enormous repercussions.'

James Lee was convinced by Clegg's argument and Pearson Longman came up with the rest of the money, which meant shooting could continue. It also meant that an epic like *Gandhi* was completed without a penny from a major Hollywood studio, which was no mean feat then or now. *Gandhi* also went on to repay substantial profits to all of its investors from Goldcrest to the various institutional sources, such as UK pension funds who had invested, and even Joe Levine who got a share of the profits for investing Paramount's money all those years before. As director and producer, Attenborough also shared in the profits. He had wagered so much for so long in terms of hard cash as well as his reputation that no one would have grudged him a penny of it. Profit-sharing in Hollywood is an ethereal, almost mythical, concept thanks to the creative accounting which exists in the movie capital of the world. A smash hit like *Batman*, for example, can gross more than $200 million at the American box office and still have a balance sheet which maintains it is well in the red. In reality only the biggest stars can claim what they call 'gross points', a share of earnings from the first dollar. Others have to console themselves with 'net points' which have all the stuff and substance of the Loch Ness Monster. *Gandhi* was not a Hollywood movie so the contracts were considerably more equitable. Nonetheless, many of those who shared in the profits of this movie did so because of the producer/director. Attenborough always insists on a share of his own profit participation being given to charity and to the crew. On *Gandhi* this meant that the widow and family of Motilal Kothari, who had died before shooting began, were still able to reap some benefit from his patience and perseverance. In addition, crew members received percentages which enabled them to buy luxuries like holiday homes and boats.

While the negotiating had continued to put the final tranche of funding in place, Attenborough was still trying to concentrate on making his movie despite all this external pressure. No matter how tense or fraught the situation became behind the scenes, none of it was ever allowed to percolate on to the floor. Ben Kingsley remembers with glowing admiration the way the director sheltered everyone else from the pressure.

'We were walking along the hotel corridor one day,' recalls the Oscar-winning actor. 'He was chatting and patting my back and telling me how well the day had gone and then he turned and went into an office for a meeting. As he went in I turned back for a moment and I happened to catch sight of him physically changing. He was like a Centurion tank, the head went down into the shoulders, the shoulders came up and he was ready for all these extraordinary characters that he had to deal with. It was like an armour-plated vehicle moving into a meeting. But for his actors he is a great patriarch and for his crew he is a general. There is a difference between the two and he switches roles very easily. One guides and enthuses, the other tells you what to do. He gives orders to his crew but never to his actors. He casts a film so well that he just places various chemical components together and he knows that even if he went out and left them alone in a room with a camera something extraordinary would happen. That's because of the quality of the scripts he accepts, the way he places his camera, and how he prepares his scenes. There are very few rehearsals, he always reminds you of the simple mandate of the scene. "This scene is to resist." "This scene is to persuade." "This scene is to grieve." "This scene is to rage." And because the underlying current of the scene is so clearly shown between Dickie and his actors, then the actors always have this wonderful mainstay against which they can moor their performance and that releases a lot of energy.'

Gandhi was the second occasion that the creative troika of Attenborough, Terry Clegg and David Tomblin had been brought together. The logistics of a film of this scale almost beggar belief. But with Attenborough at the apex and Clegg and Tomblin providing support a massive 121-day location shoot in India was completed only three days over schedule and that was because it rained during the dry season. Not even Terry Clegg's meticulous planning could legislate for that. For Terry Clegg filming in India was an organisational nightmare. India is by nature a bureaucratic nation and everything happens or does not happen depending on which piece of paper you have at the time. Many of the cast and crew have fond memories and a number have been back for holidays, but Clegg's affection is tempered by the memory of the sheer, day in, day out, paper war which had to be fought.

'What they say in India is that the British created the bureaucracy and they perfected it,' he jokes. 'When the British moved out of India the jobs they left behind were split between four or five people for the very simple reason that they had to put bread on the table for as many mouths as they could. What that meant was a lot of confusion which could only work by shuffling lots of paper around. In London if you want to shoot at the Albert Hall you don't go to the hall porter, you go to the guy who is in charge of the hall. Not in India. You start somewhere round about the bottom of the ladder and you have to work your way up paper-wise through that chain of command until you get to the right one. If you try to cut short that process they will remind you very forcibly that it's not the way things are done. It's very, very pedantic and very, very frustrating but we quickly realised that if you don't do things the Indian way then they simply don't get done.'

The co-operation of the Indian authorities was vital but Attenborough had

What we did on our holidays. Attenborough and Ben Kingsley pose for a publicity shot arranged by then director of publicity Diana Hawkins

been reluctant because of the political situation in her country at the time and because there was still opposition to the film in some quarters. But Clegg is firm in his belief that had Attenborough asked then she would have stepped in.

Gandhi is the film that Attenborough had been wanting to make for 18 years. He had had some sucess with his previous movies but it was still a massive undertaking for a man who was only going behind the camera for the fifth time. More than ever he needed the support of his old faithfuls and he got it. He brought together Clegg and David Tomblin, associate producer Michael Stanley-Evans, sound recordist Simon Kaye, cameramen Ronnie Taylor and Billy Williams, and production designer Stuart Craig. These men formed the core of his unit, the creative anchors whom he knew he could rely on to help him through the biggest directorial undertaking of his life.

'What was evident to me at that time,' recalls Terry Clegg, 'was that technically Dickie was not very proficient. In a technical sense he didn't know too much about lenses and equipment and all those things. What he did know about, which is always his strength, is that he knows how to handle actors. He knows how to get performances out of actors that nobody else can achieve. At that time I felt he relied a lot on his premier crew, David particularly but also the directors of photography and the production designer. Between them Dickie really had the best of everything, he had the best possible advice and the best possible support.

'The thing with David is that Dickie trusts him implicitly. David is so confident and so good at his job; he is simply the best assistant director in the world. On that very first day a lot of assistants would have been thrown into panic because the director was late but David actually had the first set-up virtually shot by the time Dickie got there. He had it all laid on, the action was rehearsed, he had the actors doing their bit, he just sort of took over and that's the way David works. Where they complement one another is that Dickie has a wonderful sense of scale. He can look at something and he knows what will make an impressive frame. He will know exactly what the shot will be that will make the sequence. In the 14 years since *Gandhi*, of course, he has become technically much more proficient. He knows about lenses, he knows about speed, he does get the pace right and he isn't so totally dependent on the editor. He is a much more adept technician than he ever was before.'

The one thing for which Attenborough has shown an unerring eye over the years is casting. His films are characterised by the number of 'unknown' actors who have given career-defining performances. Ben Kingsley was virtually unknown outside the London stage when he was recommended to Attenborough by the director's son, Michael. Attenborough was duly impressed by what he saw and cast him in a role which had been previously earmarked for the likes of Anthony Hopkins, John Hurt and – most bizarrely of all – Richard Burton. For Kingsley, who in his own words had 'zero status' before this picture, Attenborough's benediction meant everything.

'There is no greater feeling than walking on to a film set knowing that you are absolutely vital to the project and you are totally needed,' he says. 'If there has been a debate beforehand and you know you were not really first choice and they have to make do otherwise they don't get their money then, unless your welcome is amazingly courteous and almost disguised, you could feel uncomfortable. But to know that you are the perfect choice, the perfect chemical for that component, for that alchemy otherwise that alchemy will not work, is invaluable. You know that you are the stuff that will turn base metal into gold because the alchemist – the director – has said, "I want that in my crucible", that makes every actor feel necessary.'

In preparing for the part Kingsley lost almost 20 pounds in weight and he did 90 minutes of yoga every morning. His hotel room was transformed with giant photographs of Gandhi, he sat on straw-filled mattresses and he slept on the floor. He also, with the aid of a tutor, learned how to spin cotton. 'I remember a prop man arriving at my door and he said, "I've got your spinning wheel, Ben. Just push this button here, that starts an electric motor, and round it goes. You don't do anything, alright?" And I said, "No thank you." I had to learn to spin. If I didn't then I would have missed the vital metaphor for this man's life. For some roles you have to ride a horse, for others you have to do your own stunts and spinning was one of my stunts. I wanted to do that to please myself and it was also in a sense my contribution to the authenticity. Richard Attenborough's was 20 years of struggle and research, mine was just a few months. But when you are with a man who is passionately enthused about his subject and puts everything into it then you get swept along with the enthusiasm.'

Gandhi was a film of enormous set pieces but there were none bigger than the funeral sequence which got them into the *Guinness Book of Records*. Accounts vary of the numbers of people involved in the scene. Attenborough puts it at 350,000, others as low as 200,000. For David Tomblin, whose job it was to control them and get them to where they were supposed to be, it was 'quite a lot of people'. The scene was rehearsed and rehearsed for weeks on end but finally the rehearsals were behind them and the moment of truth had arrived. David Tomblin, the man who had pulled off the Million Dollar Hour at Nijmegen, had planned the operation meticulously and every contingency was catered for.

'It was tough,' he recalls soberly. 'We had 1,500 guards, which is one every metre on each side of the road, and I gave the instruction that once we stopped none of the crowd were to move so that we could shift the cameras. I had to work out a plan where we stopped and the cameras were moved to a different position and then we started again. This was the most nerve-wracking time, especially with those hundreds of thousands of people who were basically there for a day out. I told all of the commanders that once we stopped they must not allow anyone on to the road. So we started shooting and I said: "Stop! Move the cameras", and suddenly there were thousands of people on the road.

'I thought we were going to have big problems so I ran into the middle of them, joined their hands together and then pushed them. They thought it was a game so they were all pushing and then the crew joined in and we split that crowd like the Red Sea. Eventually we got them off the road and got things going again and allowed the cortège, which I think was 3,000 people on its own, to start off once more. By this stage I was hanging in rags and unfortunately I turned and right in the middle of the road there was a man with a camera taking a picture. I saw red and I ran down the road and picked him up and threw him bodily into the crowd. I found out later that he was one of the official photographers for the Indian Navy, which didn't go down too well. But we got through the day and we got the shot. I know it's only on the screen for a short time but it's in the mind for a long time. Most of the things I do are big shots which you only see fleetingly. I would be much happier to see a lot more of them but then it would unbalance the rest of the film.

'Something like the *Gandhi* funeral is a genuinely collaborative effort. Dickie finds people on the same wavelength and you don't need to have long discussions. You trust what they do and they trust what you do and it is a team effort in that sense. Obviously in certain areas you will have a discussion with Dickie about what he wants and then you get on with it. That's only common sense because usually the problems are large ones and you can't really say, "Stop the battle, we need to have a talk."'

David Tomblin and Terry Clegg weren't the only members of the production team to have difficulties in India. The shoot was also something of a nightmare for sound recordist Simon Kaye. Attenborough had first asked him to do *Gandhi* while they were filming *Oh! What A Lovely War.* 'He would keep telling me it was going to happen,' Kaye recalls. 'Every time he went out scouting a location he would send me a postcard back. But then when we came to do it he said to me, "There's just one problem and that is that I don't think you will be able to record a single word of usable dialogue." So I said I didn't think I wanted to do it but the more I thought about it the more I thought if it was that much of a challenge then I really wanted to do it.

'I think in the end we managed something like 75 per cent of the sound recorded on location. Background noise was the greatest problem. The scenes which were supposed to be in Jan Smuts's office were shot in a building which opened on to the Raj Path, which is a four-lane motorway. A group of us went in to check it out. There was Stuart Craig the designer, Billy Williams the director of photography, Dickie, David Tomblin and me. When we went into this place the noise was incredible. They drive on their hooters in India, they drive and they honk their horns. I sometimes wondered if their cars had any mirrors. The noise was almost unbearable and I was standing obviously looking very forlorn because it was a very big, very open office complex that Stuart was going to turn into Smuts's office. I stood there while they were talking about chairs and desks and library effects and so on and Dickie saw me. He said, "What is it, Simon? If you don't like it we won't shoot here."

'And I said, "Okay, where will we shoot if we don't shoot here?"

'Dickie said, "Well actually we've just lost the other location."

'So I said, "Okay, we shoot here." But he knows the problems of location shooting and he knows location films are never easy. There are all sorts of reasons for that. You might have a night sequence and the cameraman suddenly decides he wants a lamp through one of the windows, so you open the window and in comes the traffic noise. There are always problems but Dickie is always understanding of all of them.'

After 21 weeks of shooting *Gandhi* was finally finished on location. Perhaps the greatest achievement of the entire shoot was Terry Clegg's. He had insisted from the start, even when they didn't know if they could afford it or not, on bringing in British caterers. The consequences of an attack of food poisoning or a dodgy tummy on a shoot like *Gandhi* would have been catastrophic. Clegg says now that it was the best insurance they ever bought. In a 21-week shoot only two people lost any time through stomach upsets. The *Gandhi* unit, Terry Clegg included, left India reluctantly, in spite of its logistical headaches and its bureaucratic labyrinths. Ben Kingsley recalls Attenborough in particular being unhappy on the final day of location shooting.

'He was grumpy the way you are grumpy when there is someone you are crazy about and you don't want them to leave but they say they have to go now,' he recalls. 'Dickie is the only human being in the world who cannot disguise his emotions and on that last day in India his lower lip was sticking out like a four-year-old.'

Once the film was complete it very quickly went from *Gandhi* the movie to *Gandhi* the phenomenon. Thanks in no small measure to the efforts of Attenborough's American agent Marti Baum, who organised screenings for every major studio inside 48 hours, the film quickly became hotter than steam. With a careful release programme and unstinting support from Attenborough and his key players on the publicity circuit the film became a bona fide smash hit. Then there were the Oscars.

Up against competition, which included *ET*, *Missing* and *Tootsie*, Attenborough's movie swept the board. It won Best Film and Best Director. Ben Kingsley won Best Actor for his début performance, beating out Paul Newman, Dustin Hoffman, Jack Lemmon and Peter O'Toole, who had 26 previous nominations between them. All told, Attenborough was able to pose triumphantly with eight Oscar statuettes the following day. One of those statuettes belonged to Ben Kingsley who was happy to pose with him. But at the same time he got a rare insight into the transience of victory.

'I have a photograph of him and me,' says Kingsley, taking up the story. 'He has his arm around me and there are all those Oscars in front of us and he looks like a man who has just got to the top of the mountain and looked at the view. The picture seems to have caught him just as he is thinking about having to walk all the way down again. I think it was very hard that day, wonderful but at the same time like a full stop. Eight Oscars, full stop, and then silence. I find that picture very touching.'

There are no Oscars, of course, for the best budget or best shooting schedule so Terry Clegg had to enjoy the moment vicariously in London. Though, by common assent, if there was an award for Best Oscar party Clegg and his *Gandhi* crew would have won hands down. 'By the time we were having the party it was the following day in Los Angeles and we already knew the result, but I had arranged for Dick to talk to us all on the speaker phone. Everyone could hear him and he sounded full of himself. It wasn't until after the event that he told me that it hadn't been such plain sailing. He had been

Richard Attenborough and Diana Hawkins and their glittering prizes

told very clearly before the ceremony that *ET* was a very strong contender and that *Missing* was a dark horse. What often happens with Oscars, and *Chariots of Fire* was a case in point, is that two strong contenders split the vote and a third film can come in and get some of the big prizes. I think he felt he might get one of the two big awards and the fact that he got both was, I think, a genuine surprise to him.'

Having, in Ben Kingsley's words, climbed the mountain and realised he would have to go down the other side many directors might have felt inclined to call it a day. He had fought for 18 years to get this film made and now he had been vindicated both at the box office and at the Academy Awards. What else was there to do now? But Terry Clegg who has come to know Attenborough as well as almost anyone maintains the thought would never have entered his head. 'I think the Oscar was a signpost for him,' he elaborates. 'It really told him he was in the top league, he was the best and he could compete with anybody. My great regret is that he didn't build on that. He stayed very firmly in his role as benefactor to the British film industry and supporter of the BFI and BAFTA and all those things instead of getting on with making movies. I think now that he has retired from all of that he suddenly realises he's a bit short of time to make all the films he wants to make.'

A Chorus of Disapproval

There were a number of problems in choosing the follow-up project to *Gandhi* especially in the light of its spectacular success. How do you follow something like that? As a film-maker I like to keep my options open. I think it would be very sad if I was constrained to a particular form of biography or a particular subject in biography and I would dread if every movie had to have a message or have some social relevance. I don't think *Chaplin*, for example, is a message film by a hundred miles. It certainly has attitudes and it has revelations but it's not a protest against colonialism, which *Gandhi* was. But a film like *A Chorus Line* I did because I'm a ham. It's like the old circus pony: you throw the sawdust down in front of him and round he goes. I can't resist a subject like *A Chorus Line*. *Chaplin* is the same. It's showbusiness, it's movies, its the glitz and glamour but just like *A Chorus Line*, it's the unknown, it's the backstage, the other side of the coin and that's what fascinates me.

It was my agent Marti Baum's idea that I should do *A Chorus Line* after *Gandhi*, I think out of a sort of pragmatism about getting too involved with pictures with strong social messages. The attraction was that it was a great musical. *A Chorus Line* is one of the great classic musicals – if you weren't doing *Oklahoma* or *Guys and Dolls* or *My Fair Lady* then the musical to do was *A Chorus Line*. I loved it because each of the 16 kids in varying degrees had the opportunity of developing their characters and providing a roundness to the element that they contributed to the overall thing. So there was the wonderful smell of the greasepaint, the razzamatazz of the musicals which I absolutely adored, as well as the theatricality of the whole thing. In addition to that, you had the fact that, no matter how far the musical had developed to the point of *Oklahoma*, the fact was that parts in musicals were in large measure cardboard characters. Whereas in *A Chorus Line* the parts were

An anxious Attenborough and his cast and crew check playback on *A Chorus Line*

daring and bold and innovative, they were wonderful and so were the performances from this young cast. And the American critics were outrageous.

Even if they did hate what I'd done and thought that the concept was a total misjudgment, to let 16 babies go out with the bathwater was criminal. They just totally ignored them and it was a scandalous thing to do because they were marvellous. There were 16 performances of exquisite judgment from those kids, they worked like crazy and the critics totally ignored their skills. They didn't give two lines to the cast because the argument had always been: 'It should have been Fosse', or something like that. That just makes me furious. Happily, in the UK there were some smashing reviews for the cast but the Americans simply ignored them. They didn't say they were bad, they just didn't give a thought for them and these youngsters had no champion until Clive Barnes came along and ripped the critics to pieces.

I knew that the reviews would not be good but what I had not anticipated was the degree or the extent. I knew that we were in for trouble. I knew right from the word go that it was a risk and that people like Bob Fosse and Mike

Nichols said it was not possible and announced that it shouldn't be done. Much as I adored the show – and I really did adore the show – I think I was seduced because I would really almost rather do a musical than anything. I knew it was a terrible risk but I didn't think they would be quite so vitriolic and, of course, they were wrong. There are a number of occasions when I think critics are right. I think they were wrong with *Chaplin* but not to the same extent – however, there are criticisms of *Chaplin* which are justified. I think you could perhaps argue that the concept of shooting *A Chorus Line* as I did was wrong, you should never have done it that way, you should never perhaps have stayed in the theatre. But to say it was badly executed was just not correct. The kids were wonderful and Clive Barnes, the man who was known as the Butcher of Broadway, wrote an article defending them which ran on the front page of his newspaper. He rode in and crucified all the film critics, he said they knew nothing about it. He said: 'I am a dance critic, I know', and I think he actually said it was the best dance movie he had ever seen. And for Clive Barnes who was not the film critic to persuade his editor that he should have the space to flay all the other critics in a way made me feel a bit better, it lifted me. But by this stage the film had been on for two weeks and the damage had been done.

I'm not sure that *A Chorus Line* isn't technically the best film I've made. The sad thing was that at the end of the day the picture was slaughtered in America and was an absolute disaster at the box office because of its terrible reviews. Maybe they thought it ought to have been something totally different but I do feel in some measure they were very angry that a limey should march on to Broadway and tamper with one of their icons. I think it was more than most people in America could endure. I have had bad reviews before as an actor – one said of *Brighton Rock:* 'Richard Attenborough's Pinky is as close to Graeme Green's character as Mickey Mouse is to Greta Garbo.' You'd have to go a long way to get a worse review than that. But even if they argue passionately that what you have made is untrue or not right or ill conceived then okay, but to be a nothing in terms of a review makes you want to die, you want to jump off the roof. If you make the films that I want to make then you know that they don't conform to what the normal studio programme requires and the moment you make one which is a flop – and I have made a number which have been flops – then the difficulty of raising the finance for the next movie is very considerable.

I think that my being British had a lot to do with the reviews, they were angered at what they saw as sheer cheek and effrontery. But I also believe the success of *Gandhi* and the awards rivalry between *Gandhi* and *ET* may have played its part in the critical reception of *A Chorus Line*. I don't think that by any means all the New York critics were in favour of *Gandhi*. I believe that there were quite a number, obviously a minority but nonetheless quite a number, who disapproved of giving me the New York Critics Award. This award, let's face it, as far as film-makers are concerned, is as prestigious as any other award that you can get. Once they decide that you get it, then all the signatures appear on your scroll. I know that there were a number of critics

Attenborough rehearses a scene with Yamil Borges from *A Chorus Line*

there who had given *Gandhi* bad reviews. There were a number of critics consequently who I think were prejudiced against me and whatever I was going to do next, they were annoyed that the majority had forced them into their position of giving me an award they didn't perhaps agree with.

There was one other incident which may have played a part and I can't remember now why I did it, but I went to pick up an award for David Lean in between *Gandhi* and *A Chorus Line* for *A Passage to India*. I was the only person who was in New York who was vaguely British and I sang 'Colonel Bogey' – the risqué version – to the New York critics, which may not have gone down very well. Other people did egg me on but I still don't know why I did it. But that's an aside. I do think the fact of this limey tinkering with one of their icons was unacceptable. I'm sure also that the fact that two of their absolutely top, renowned, proven, established movie-makers in the person of Bob Fosse and Mike Nichols had publicly said the show was unfilmable also went against us. This '*Gandhi* backlash', if you like, had manifested itself previously. After the film had been a huge success articles started to appear which criticised it for what it wasn't. But, that said, it was the spirit of the vitriol and the unanimity of the hostility in New York which was staggering. Yet there are a vast number of people who have copies of *A Chorus Line* who play it over and over. They just find it to be a wonderful movie. I caught the end of it on television recently – where they are all lined up at the end and some have parts in the show and others haven't – and it reminded me how good they all were. I think it was the happiest film I ever worked on. Even now, after all these years, there are people who will stick their head above the parapet and defend it. Mickey Rooney, of all people, told me a couple of years ago that *A Chorus Line* was one of his favourite musicals.

In spite of the reviews and the box-office failure of *A Chorus Line* I never doubted I would bounce back. I always bounce back. I am very rarely totally cast down, people tell me it's very worrying when I am. I suppose in a way it has something to do with being an actor. And in a theatre actor in particular, being depressed by reviews is completely out of the question. You simply can't be affected because you have to give a performance every night. You can open in a play and you can have the reviewers tell you that you are absolutely rubbish – and I'm not one of those people who will not read their reviews, because I do – but you still have to go on and do the play. But I don't think that in itself is sufficient explanation. I am an optimist, I am a total optimist about almost anything. I don't mean that I count my chickens, I don't mean that, on the contrary I'm usually very sceptical in terms of my achievements. But I am an optimist to the extent that I believe that things will work out and I believe that with enough care, attention, commitment, energy, unflagging determination and I suppose even ruthlessness things will work out. I suppose the word ruthless in some degree might be applied to me if I am scrupulously honest. I am not conscious, with one or two exceptions, of actually putting people down in that regard. I would never hurt anybody, well I might but I would bitterly regret it afterwards. But I am fairly tough and when I say ruthless I mean it in the sense of my determination to achieve what I want to achieve. I don't mean ruthless in the sense of self-aggrandisement or in terms of creating a private fortune or something, I mean ruthless perhaps like Charlie Chaplin in my determination to achieve a certain level of work and going to almost any length to arrive at that point. I would be greatly distressed if people thought that I trampled over people, that I abused people in personal relationships or by being cruel or thoughtless. That would distress me. But I think there is a degree of toughness and determination and I suppose that if you do things that I want to do which are not easy, which do not conform and do not fit necessarily into commercial pigeon-holes, then your life can be a relentless pursuit of what you want to do. *Chaplin*, for example, didn't take the time that *Gandhi* did but it was by no means an easy picture and without that sort of determination you couldn't do it.

The Glass is Half-Empty

Hollywood hates surprises. That's not quite true. It doesn't mind the sort of surprise where a *Wayne's World* or a *Ghost* comes out of left field and goes on to be a colossal smash. What it hates is the other sort of surprise. The sort of surprise where a *Last Action Hero* belly flops at the box office, leaving the studio in the cart to the tune of millions of dollars. So the industry does whatever it can to prevent the sort of nasty shock which that kind of surprise can bring.

In America, unlike Britain, film publicity and marketing people usually know what the reviews are going to be like well in advance of publication. There are a number of reasons for this. It's partly because film critics, like the rest of the world, want their 15 minutes of fame, they all want to see their name underneath that glowing 12-word review on the movie poster or in the newspaper ad. It's also because relationships between film publicists and journalists tend to be a lot closer in the United States. It is not uncommon for a film reviewer to send a copy of his review to the film company after he has written it but before it is published. In addition, when a major studio has a press screening for a big movie it is normal practice to ring round the following day to get critical reaction or a quote for the ad – sometimes both. With all these safety nets in place there are plenty of fail-safes to alert a company well in advance to an embarrassing flop and allow a damage-limitation exercise to swing into place.

Unfortunately, with *A Chorus Line* none of these systems worked. The basic reason was that although Embassy Pictures was a major company it wasn't a *major* major company so it didn't have that kind of publicity and marketing operation. At that time Attenborough's director of publicity was his long-term friend and ally Diana Hawkins. They first met when she was a teenager in the publicity department at Rank. She had gone on to become his personal assistant and after five years in that role she returned to her true calling when Attenborough asked her to be director of publicity on *Gandhi*. She served the same function on *A Chorus Line* and *Cry Freedom* before becoming an associate producer on *Chaplin* and finally co-producer of *Shadowlands*. She was with Attenborough when it became obvious they were in trouble with *A Chorus Line*.

'On *Gandhi* we were working with Columbia and we had known in advance what the reviews were going to be and in that case the vibes were good,' she recalls. 'For *A Chorus Line* we were in New York and we were working with Lois Smith, who handles Robert Redford's publicity. She is an old friend and Dick had worked with her before and admired her tremendously. We went out to do radio interviews to promote the movie which was opening a few nights later and Dick kept telling me to phone Lois to get news of what was going on and how the movie was being received. I knew from talking to her and from a kind of publicist's subtext that it wasn't going well. Dick was very bouncy but this is very much how we operate as a duo. He is always the optimist and for him the

Attenborough and Janet Jones on *A Chorus Line*. He referred to her throughout as 'Ugly' for obvious reasons

glass is always half-full while I am eternally looking for the down side. He says I'm a pessimist but I would rather think of myself as someone who prefers to think the worst, works out how to deal with it, then when it happens I am comfortable with it. Dick always believes that the best is going to happen and in this case when it appeared that was not so, it fell to me to tell him. "Dick," I said, "I think we are in a bad situation here." So we started making more calls and examining the situation further and the more we looked at it the more obvious it became that we were going to get stinking reviews.'

Different people react to reviews in different ways. Some refuse to read them at all, some read them but ignore them, others read them and take every word to heart for better or worse. Attenborough comes somewhere in the middle. He reads them and he tries to understand them and work out what prompted them.

'There's no doubt that he was upset,' says Diana Hawkins. 'I've been with him in other situations like that. He doesn't shout, he doesn't rant, he doesn't rave, he is genuinely hurt. As far as I can remember, he did initially take the reviews very personally. But what I think he was most hurt about was that they were criticising the script and the direction but in doing that they didn't give any of the cast good reviews. Dick believes, or at least I think he hopes, that a critic might say: "Okay the script was lousy but so and so did a great job with the material to hand." *A Chorus Line* was so important to all of those kids, they all hoped that their careers would take off because of it. It's a really strange thing about *A Chorus Line* but I don't think anyone came out of that show and built their career on it. None of them became a star. Michael Douglas was already established because by that time he had already produced *One Flew Over the Cuckoo's Nest*. He may have been in something of a trough at the time of *A Chorus Line* but he was still up there as far as Hollywood was concerned.

'In a situation like that all of the ebullience is simply knocked out of Dick. Because he is such an optimist and because he hadn't prepared for it I think he was totally shattered for the first 24 hours. Only once have I seen him more depressed, so depressed I was quite worried. After Labour lost the 1992 General Election it took him several weeks to get to the point where he could function properly again. He is a friend and enormous admirer of Neil Kinnock. To this day he's never got over it completely.

'He takes his politics very seriously. Very few people know it, but he was offered and declined a working Peerage in the Resignation Honours immediately following the election. He felt obliged to turn down this political appointment because he knew that he couldn't attend the House of Lords regularly representing the Opposition and make movies. The peerage which he accepted a year later is different. That was awarded in recognition of his unflagging support of cinema – British cinema in particular – and his long life in public service. He's not obliged to work or be present for every major vote although he does sit on the Labour benches and, if I know Dick, he'll be there whenever he's not making a film.'

Attenborough's Socialism, like most of the qualities he has which people find hard to understand, comes from his parents who were very early members of the Labour Party. According to Diana Hawkins, Attenborough is the only person she knows who never rebelled against his parents. Quite the opposite. From his father he got his love of soccer, of paintings, and of music. Also from his father comes almost a veneration of learning, coupled with an abiding regret that he never went to university. From his mother, who must have been quite a woman, comes his love of theatre and acting and the resolute conviction that you have to stand up and be counted.

'Another thing he gets from his parents is an old-fashioned courtliness,' says Diana Hawkins. 'He's the only man I know who always raises his hat to women when he meets them in the street and always writes his bread-and-butter letters promptly and by hand. He used to apologise if he swore in a lady's presence, but I notice he's stopped doing that recently.'

Attenborough's unpaid activities are a constant source of good-natured teasing between him and his production partner. Though she does get annoyed, and probably with justification, when people take him for granted, loading him with work which extends his day beyond the point which anyone else would find reasonable. 'When we're not shooting he starts at nine in the morning, sometimes earlier,' she explains, 'and rarely finishes his paperwork and his phone calls before 11 at night. When we're shooting he often does a 16 or even an 18-hour day, six days a week. And you can guarantee he is the only person on the set who never uses the chair with his name on it. He is always on his feet. And on Sunday, which is a rest day for the shooting crew, he usually works a few hours with the editor.'

This is a workload which would cripple a younger man but for Attenborough, at the age of 71, this is his slimmed-down schedule after divesting himself of many of his outside activities. It is not unknown for him to get up at six in the morning, take a three-and-a-half-hour Concorde flight to New York and then work a full day on East Coast time, meaning he is effectively on the go for 24 hours at a time.

Diana Hawkins, along with David Tomblin and Terry Clegg – his trusted associates – are the ones who most often bear the brunt of the director's infrequent blow-ups. Most of the time, as he has explained himself earlier, it's a means to an end. Occasionally, though, it can be the genuine article.

'One of the great things about Dick though is that he never harbours grudges,' says Hawkins. 'Over the years I have known a number of instances where people have done him down or let him down. Yet not once have I ever known him to take any form of revenge. It's like his anger. When he's in a real rage I call it "the purple poppy-eyed screamers", and believe me they are terrifying. But if you mention whatever it was that brought it on about a week later he genuinely doesn't remember. It's out of his system, gone, forgotten.

'He is also a remarkably generous man and I don't know where this phenomenal generosity comes from but it is truly phenomenal. Since he began to make real money with the success of *Gandhi* he's donated almost £1 million of his fees to various charities. And on every film we make he gives a large chunk of his own profit participation away to the crew. He doesn't have to do that and to my knowledge other producer/directors don't do it. On top of that there

Attenborough looks on as Terrence Mann and Alyson Reed perform a key scene in
A Chorus Line

must be hundreds of instances of private charity. One of the New York actresses in *A Chorus Line* needed an operation to make sure she would be able to have children in later life. She couldn't afford it but Dick brought her to London, put her in a private clinic, found the best gynaecologist available and paid for the lot. Nobody knew that but the girl, his wife Sheila, and the people who worked closely with him. He doesn't trumpet those things and neither do the recipients, but they are legion.'

The man who recommended that Attenborough take on *A Chorus Line* was his long-time Hollywood agent and close personal friend Marti Baum. As one of the most respected agents in the business, he and Attenborough form a formidable partnership but he had advised his client to do *A Chorus Line* in the wake of *Gandhi* to avoid directorial type-casting as much as anything else. Even now Baum remains a staunch defender of the movie. 'I don't care what the reviews said, I think it is a fine picture,' he says, emphatically. 'The anger of the critics was based on the fact that they were comparing it to the show. They felt the show, which had run for ten or 12 years, was better than the movie. I think it is a very good film and I think that without question it gave Michael Douglas the chance which pushed him forward into stardom. Up until then Michael was a small actor playing small movie parts coming off a successful television series. It was his first big break and Dickie's perception in recognising his potential was quite extraordinary. Michael Douglas is now a $15-million-a-picture star.'

Like Attenborough, Marti Baum believes a lot of criticism was motivated purely and simply by xenophobia. How dare an Englishman come and make a movie about an American institution, especially when their own favourite cinematic sons had said it couldn't be done? But he also believes there was an element of payback for Attenborough's previous success. 'Don't forget *A Chorus Line* was his next picture after *Gandhi*,' he says. 'For *Gandhi* they couldn't praise him highly enough and they lifted him to the skies. And with *A Chorus Line* I believe they took pleasure in dashing him to the ground. It's a perverse thing that happens with human nature but it's true. I think it applies in this case and I think they are unfairly and unnecessarily and wrongly critical of a very fine effort.'

It's perfectly natural for both Attenborough and Marti Baum to look for motives in the harshest reviews the director had ever had, for a film which he believed at that time was his best to date. The conspiracy theory of film criticism is a seductive one but it holds little charm for Diana Hawkins. 'If you are a star actor or a star director then I think in trying to make sense of the ups and downs of show business you probably look for patterns and you search for motives,' she agrees. 'I think Dick had thought there was an element of conspiracy and probably still does. I'm not at all sure that people do sit around in bars or wherever and say: "We've built him up for *Gandhi* now we're going to smash him." I think if you have a major achievement people tend to look at you more critically and they probably examine what you do more closely but I don't think there was any kind of conspiracy. I think if you are the artist it probably looks that way to you because even in Britain we build people up and knock them down but I don't think it tends to happen that way. It may be a

Attenborough rehearses his dancers in *A Chorus Line*

factor, it may be part of the reason, but the simple fact is that nobody can make hits all of the time. Inevitably, you go into everything believing it is going to be wonderful but it doesn't always work out like that.'

It's ironic that the reviews for *A Chorus Line* were so harsh since the film features Attenborough's most adventurous direction to date. He has criticised himself for not showing as much flair as he might in some of his films but in *A Chorus Line* he moved his camera with panache and élan. The theory was simple. If you make the decision to keep the film in the theatre then the camera has to move where the characters can not. Attenborough sends it prowling through the wings and soaring into the galleries to keep the audience constantly engaged by what is happening within the confines of the proscenium arch.

'Dick believes that *A Chorus Line* is his greatest achievement as a director in terms of the use of the camera,' says Hawkins. 'He put a lot of effort into thinking about the camera and the various patterns of camera movements. I don't know that he had done that before and I don't know that he necessarily did it in his next film, *Cry Freedom*. But I'm also certain that it wasn't because he was retrenching because of having had his fingers burned by the reviews. With *A*

Chorus Line he knew he was going to be shooting inside that theatre for weeks and weeks on end so he thought very carefully about saving things up and he worried about repetition. He always knew in his own mind, for example, that he could only ever have one tracking shot across the whole chorus line on stage and that had to be the end sequence. So, having taken away one very obvious major way of showing that stage, he was then forced to be very inventive.'

Attenborough's solution was to resort once again to the giant Louma crane which had been used to good effect to provide some devastating 360-degree pans in *Gandhi*. One of the great talking-points among the crew was what came to be known as 'the pigeon shot'. At the start of the movie Attenborough told the camera operator that he wanted the camera to start in close on the dancers and then come up and up and back until it looks as though it might burst through the roof of the theatre. The camera operator in question is alleged to have told him that 'the only way you'll get that shot is if you attach the camera to a fucking pigeon and let it fly away'. Nonetheless, he got the shot thanks to the Louma crane, which was the only way of getting the speed and manoeuvrability he needed to capture exactly what he wanted.

Michael Douglas and Richard Attenborough on *A Chorus Line*

After having to go into battle for his leading man in one way or another in four of his first five movies, Attenborough must have felt at the very least a sense of déjà vu when he once again met opposition to his casting decisions. This time the problem was Michael Douglas as Zack, the tyrannical director of the show for which the young hopefuls are auditioning.

'I don't know that Dick thought of anyone but Michael for the role,' recalls Diana Hawkins. 'He said to Embassy, "I want Michael Douglas to play Zack", and they said, "Michael Douglas couldn't act his way out of a paper bag." Not only is that patently untrue, it's a horrible thing to say about anyone. I think that once again we got to a point where Dick said, "If I can't have Michael then we can forget the whole thing." It doesn't happen that often but he is a great believer and if he believes in something and he also believes that doing anything else will compromise the whole picture then he will take a stand the way he did for Michael and the way he did for Robert Downey in *Chaplin*. That's typical of the sort of courage he shows in making his movies. It's a card you can't play very often but when you play it you have to be able to live with the consequences, as he did with *Chaplin*. You can't turn round and say, "Oh my God, I didn't really mean that." You have to say, as he did, "That's it, we're out. We're gone." Then you have to live with it when they call the movie off.

'That is a rare thing for anyone to do in Hollywood,' she continues. 'The other thing he does that they are not used to is that he is prepared to put his money where his mouth is. For instance, there was a moment when we still had *Chaplin* at Universal and they said that the picture was too expensive. We told them we had pared the budget to the bone and it would not work if we did not have what we believed to be that minimum amount for costumes and settings and crowds. They maintained it was still too expensive and after a lot of pressure from them Dick eventually said, "Okay, I will cut my salary by half." He is prepared to put his own money into things.'

Like Diana Hawkins, Marti Baum has experience of Attenborough dipping into his own pocket to finance his pictures. On *Gandhi*, for example, Attenborough himself initially paid to hire Terry Clegg as production executive while the finance was still being negotiated.

'*Shadowlands* was a tough one too,' recalls Marti Baum. 'The money wasn't finally going to flow until all the papers were signed and there were eight sets of lawyers involved getting *Shadowlands* closed. At this stage Dickie was funding the picture out of his own pocket and I kept saying to him, "Don't worry we're going to get this to work." But when we passed the $3 million mark he said to me, "If you don't get this to work I'm out of business. The house goes, the paintings go, everything." I said, "Dickie, trust me we will get this to work out," and we did.'

The most coveted thing in Hollywood is a 'pay or play' deal. It is in effect a licence to print money for the talent whose services are so in demand that the studio is willing to pay for those services whether the movie ever gets made or not. Attenborough could get a pay or play deal tomorrow almost anywhere but simply doesn't want one. When a film is at the development stage he is a great believer in not taking anyone else's money for it to avoid ending up being committed to making something he doesn't really like. He needs to be free to say that if the picture is to be made then it has to be made his way, and taking the cash would compromise that. Pay or play deals in Attenborough's book aren't fair to either him or the studio making the offer. Naturally, if the film is made then he will recover the money he spent in the start-up phase from the budget, but if the film isn't made then he loses and he is prepared to take that risk to preserve his integrity.

One of the reasons for this has to do with the change from being a director for hire to a producer and originator of his own material. That, in turn, has to do with his experiences on *A Bridge Too Far* and *Magic*. 'I think he is a different film-maker after *Gandhi* than he was as a director for hire,' says Diana Hawkins. 'I think that is because his experience with Joe Levine was so bruising and so damaging that he really vowed not to put himself in that position again if he could possibly help it. Of course, he was effectively a director for hire on *A Chorus Line*, although I think he would have liked to have been the producer. We did have our ups and downs with the producers but we get on very well with them and we have spoken with them since about the possibility of doing other things with them. There were arguments, strong arguments, but nothing that wouldn't make it work.'

The one thing that all of his collaborators – Diana Hawkins, Terry Clegg, David Tomblin, Anthony Hopkins, and Marti Baum – know about Richard Attenborough is that he loves to be in charge. There is nothing he likes better than having total responsibility for what is going on around him. That includes his work with charities such as the Muscular Dystrophy Group, of which he has been president for 30 years, as well as industry bodies, such as the British Film Institute and Channel 4 Television both of which he chaired for over a decade. Although over the past two years he has effectively withdrawn himself from that type of work, it did make enormous demands on his time. 'I think those of us on the film side of Dick's life begrudge the amount of time that he spends on other things,' admits Diana Hawkins. 'It's what I call his "Chairman of London" syndrome. For instance, these days during the lunch break on the set he likes to have a quick bowl of soup and then a sleep because he is one of those lucky people who can drop off for ten or 15 minutes and then wake up recharged. We all feel he has much greater energy because of that but if somebody gets on the phone from one of his organisations during lunch then he can come back with additional cares and worries. He's very good at shutting them out but we do resent it.

'He's been made a lot of offers to run studios – Olivier asked him to take over the National Theatre and Charles Bludhorn asked him to take charge of production at Paramount – but he doesn't want any of that. We've talked a lot about why we don't have some kind of development programme, we always seem to be juggling four balls in the air, but he just wants to do one movie and be besotted by it. He is at his happiest when he is on the floor directing.

'But Dick never regrets any of the time he spends doing other things, he never regrets the movie he's made or the movies he might have made. Something is done and it's over, then it's time to move on and make the next picture.'

Freedom of Expression

I suppose *Cry Freedom* in terms of its political content, is a distillation of everything that I learned at my parents' knee about decency and humanity and the way people should be treated. I do have this yen, this desire, this need to express conviction whether it be pro or con. Why I have it I don't quite know but I have it nonetheless and this is why I believe I will enjoy my time in the House of Lords. I have this requirement to be able to express very deep feelings about certain things and I remember as a young man being totally shattered by apartheid. I flew with South Africans; they were part of the crew that I flew with in the war. I distinctly remember that the navigator was a South African. I remember being sledge hammered, crushed, when this dreadful policy was adopted. So right from 1948 I loathed the apartheid system. I really loathe prejudice of any kind, including all the most obvious, and I found the South African situation deeply distressing. So given all of that, the opportunity of doing *Cry Freedom* was something which I could in no way pass over.

We were having a crew screening of *A Chorus Line* in London and Donald Woods was introduced to me by a friend of mine called Norman Spencer whom I had known since 1941 when he was on *In Which We Serve*. Norman said to me, 'I'd like you to read this book.' It was Donald's book on Steve Biko called *Asking for Trouble*, and I could immediately see its possibilities. So what you have to understand is that *Cry Freedom* didn't come out of any kind of knee-jerk response to the savaging *A Chorus Line* had had in America, it wasn't a question of withdrawing into the sort of movie-making people supposed I knew about. Although America had been dreadful, the reaction to *A Chorus Line* in the UK had been very good, it was also huge in Germany where it ran for a year. So it wasn't solace, it was purely a question of conviction.

I think there is no doubt that *Cry Freedom* was ahead of its time, which is possibly why it failed at the American box office. There was one tragic misunderstanding which my co-producer Diana Hawkins only hit on recently. It had never occurred to me before and I think with hindsight she is absolutely right. This was a marvellous, real movie with again wonderful performances from Kevin Kline, Denzel Washington and Penelope Wilton. Denzel had done very little except television before that. I asked him to come to New York and meet me and I remember him standing, leaning against a piece of furniture as we talked. He knew nothing about South Africa, nothing about Steve Biko, he just stood there and he had this style, this presence, this confidence. He's a terrific guy and he takes meticulous care. He doesn't believe that you just go on and ad-lib a few lines or mumble in a corner and that's a performance. As for Kevin, I'd seen him do *Hamlet* in New York and he was wonderful. But, as Diana pointed out, the tragedy was that we had a good film and couldn't think of an equally good title for a long time. However, because we couldn't come up with a title it came to be known as 'The Biko Story'. So the presumption was that was indeed what it was, that it was the life story of Steve Biko.

It wasn't, of course – far from it. It was a film about a black man and a white man and their friendship and the demonstration of the faith that they each had in the other. It was also ultimately, because those were the circumstances, the extent to which the white man was prepared to sacrifice everything in order to tell the story of the black man. So it wasn't 'The Biko Story', and what an idiotic thing it would have been to have attempted to make a film about the life of Steve Biko. In the first place it was far too early and in the second place there was no way you could do the research that was required because of the repressions of the system which still existed. I was absolutely firm in my determination not to show anything on screen which we did not know had absolutely happened in real life.

Cry Freedom was a terribly important document at that time and again we had this tragedy about some of the reviews, I don't understand it, unless of course, as Barry Norman of the BBC once said, you want to criticise a film which the film-maker never intended to make in the first place. For me that attitude was never more exemplified than with *Cry Freedom*. The reviews didn't attack the film and say it was unreal, they didn't say it was badly performed, nor did they say it was over prejudiced. What they did say was that it was not the film that should have been made. 'The film died the moment Steve Biko did,' they said. 'Surely a film about Steve Biko should have him there throughout. Once he dies the film is finished. It's a film of two parts.' Of course it was a film of two parts and if one of your two principal characters dies it splits the film in two. But how idiotic and how ill-judged of them to take that simplistic attitude. Doubtless these same sort of problems will be faced when they ultimately make a film about Mandela. Incidentally, when they do make that movie I hope to God that it is made by an African.

We were not able to shoot in South Africa for obvious reasons. However, it was absolutely essential to make as credible a replica in terms of

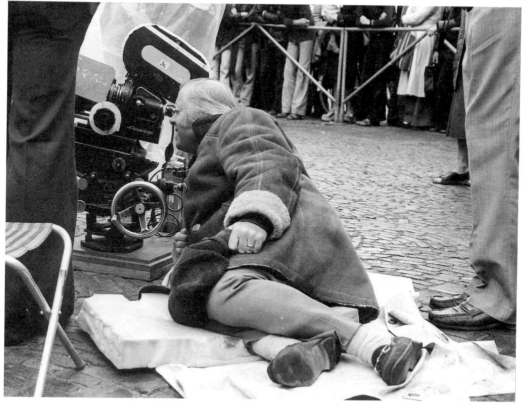

Attenborough checking a shot

geographical reality so that no matter wherever we went and no matter however we did it, it should be absolutely acceptable as South Africa. In the end we chose Zimbabwe. It was because of my profound confidence in our production designer Stuart Craig, who I first worked with on *A Bridge Too Far*, that I felt that he would, both in terms of his doggedness and his artistic creative vision, provide something which no one would ever deny.

It was also on *Cry Freedom* that Diana, Terry and I were joined by two other people who have become part of our creative core: the editor Lesley Walker and the script supervisor Nikki Clapp. Lesley's skill is the understanding of what is potentially there in the various takes. We seemed almost instinctively to agree on the tempo and intensity of sequence after sequence. A director, of course, can make the most appalling errors on the shooting floor by omitting an absolutely vital shot or simply getting something wrong, inhibiting the way it will ultimately cut together. You are saved over and over again by continuity girls of the calibre of Nikki Clapp. In terms of our core crew there are two others who are not there during shooting but I wouldn't dream of making a film without them. One of them is Jonathan Bates, the son of the great H.E. Bates, who is our sound editor on picture after picture. The other is Gerry Humphries who is without question, in my opinion, the finest dubbing mixer in the world. He is also one of the directors of Twickenham Studios where we always do all of our post-production.

During our time on location in Zimbabwe our entire unit was under armed guard. I had two of them looking after me all the time but one really mustn't exaggerate that. I do think that the South African government at that time was as repressive as it ever was, other than during the ghastly massacres which have taken place over the years. They were ruthless in their attacks on the film even to the extent of fabricating another movie which was ostensibly in place and giving approval to it as an obstacle to us. They said they were going to tell the true story and their machinations were indicative of the extent to which they were determined to stop our film. Twice or three times the security services halted what amounted to sabotage units which came across the border – this is all documented – and so it was a very strange feeling to be directing under the supervision of armed bodyguards. But in a way when you're committed to making a movie there are so many other problems that need concern you. There are so many other obstacles that you have to overcome that if the situation isn't present in front of you, as it were, you tend to ignore it. The one occasion when I really couldn't ignore it was when they were setting up the Steve Biko funeral scene. There were going to be thousands of people and I was planning out the logistics of the funeral with David Tomblin. I was aware of the dangers then because we were walking across this huge empty area. I was conscious of the two guards, one in front of me and one behind, and I suddenly felt that if someone had got a rifle or something they could have knocked me off.

The worst experiences, by far the worst, were when Sheila and I went ahead of the film into South Africa. I really was genuinely frightened. I'll never forget that, never. There was one occasion when we were in the middle of the Orange Free State and we stopped off at a garage for petrol. I went into the toilet and I was followed by two huge Afrikaners who made it pretty clear what they thought of me and what they intended to do about it. I admit that I was scared then and I'm still not sure how I got out of it – we were in the middle of nowhere. But the place had a set of those swinging bat-wing doors like in a Western and I think I feinted in one direction and went in the other and got out. I was frightened then and I was even more scared when we were leaving South Africa and the police or whoever they were bumped the car all the way to the airport. Frightened, I suppose, is an exaggeration, but boy was I ever glad to see the livery of that British Airways plane and get out of there.

It was the conviction which led me to make movies like *Cry Freedom* which ultimately persuaded me to give up acting, until recently, and concentrate full time on directing. I was being offered parts which had begun to pall, and to spend your life playing manic depressives or panicky sailors on the lower decks of Her Majesty's Navy should not properly be the height of one's ambition. There are certain things I want to do and this goes back to why I enjoy biography. The thing about biography is that it carries with it an element of the achievement of that particular person and very often that person has things which he cares about very passionately which he or she wishes to examine or challenge or question. I suppose I am that kind of a person in that I like to challenge things and I want to pose certain questions and I want to protest about certain things. The medium in which I choose to do that is the movies. If I am purely an actor then my position is interpretive although obviously I have the ability to accept or reject a particular script. A particular part can in some degree illuminate that particular personality or elements in that personality. But at the end of the day you are engaged to interpret that part in that script. By directing you select not only the fundamental subject matter but you select the starting point from which you examine that subject matter. You also decide, albeit arbitrarily, but you do decide by inclusion or exclusion the elements in that story which you want to emphasise. These are the elements you think are worthy of attention and which you think will provide entertainment in a cinema for two or two-and-a-half hours. Only by producing and directing can you do that, you can't do it as an actor. Therefore, once I got that taste, once I got excited, movies as such became to me much more satisfying if I was in that position rather than merely as an actor. With all of the many things that I care about very deeply or the great many things that I want to say I have to accept that I can't write and I don't paint or compose. I'm not an academic so I can't deal with them in that forum, but I'm not satisfied merely to be an actor. Marvellous though it is to be an actor, it is essentially an interpretive art. Directing a movie, making a movie with the script that you want, with the cast that you have chosen, with the crew who you have assembled is a gift from the Gods. It is simply the most magical opportunity anyone can imagine.

Under Armed Guard

One of the first people Richard Attenborough cast in *Chaplin* was Kevin Kline. When he asked the droll Mid-Westerner, whether he would do the movie or not, Attenborough received the reply: 'Dickie, you know I would follow you into crocodile-infested waters, in fact I already have.' This was not simply a show of theatrical extravagance on Kline's part, he had indeed waded through waters inhabited by deadly reptiles during the filming of *Cry Freedom*.

The movie is the story of white South African newspaperman Donald Woods and his friendship with black activist Steve Biko. Through that friendship Woods' eyes were opened to what was going on in his country in the Seventies. Their friendship also led to Woods being placed under house arrest. In the end, when Biko died at the hands of the security forces, Woods risked everything to escape from South Africa with his family and tell Biko's story to the world. Kline was playing Woods, the splendid Penelope Wilton was playing his wife, Wendy, and Denzel Washington was to play Steve Biko.

The most gripping part of the movie is where Woods, dressed as a priest, attempts to make good his escape in an operation planned with split-second precision. If anything went wrong then he would not make the appointed rendezvous with his family and would have either to go back or leave without them, knowing he might never see them again. It was during this escape sequence that the cultured Kline encountered the creatures he was more used to seeing as shoes and handbags in the up-market department stores of New York.

'We were on the Zambesi River right above the Victoria Falls,' he remembers. 'In fact you could hear the falls roaring in the background. I flew over the area in one of those light-aircraft tours the day before we filmed the scene. People had said there were a lot of crocodiles there and the pilot took great delight in pointing them out to me as we flew over. I saw one of them scurrying into the water just a few hundred yards from where we were due to shoot the following day. I could see our trucks and I could see the crocodiles. I had also been told, however, that we had two men in a boat with a high-powered rifle should any crocodiles be spotted while we were filming.

'The crocodiles really weren't the worst part, the worst part was the fear of bilharzia, a nasty tropical disease we had all had leaflets about. We'd been told about avoiding water that wasn't running at a good clip, and on the day the water where we were shooting was rather still. I was more concerned about that – it's a terrible parasitic infection in which the parasites congregate in your kidneys – so I was wearing a wet-suit for all-over protection. It wasn't until after the scene when I said, "What were those two guys doing in the canoe?" that they told me they had in fact been playing cards while we were filming. They did have a high-powered rifle with them but they were otherwise engaged. Had I been attacked, I'm sure they would have got off a couple of shots before the crocodile started on my other leg – always assuming they didn't have a really good hand.'

Kevin Kline knew of and was impressed by Richard Attenborough's reputation as an actor from films he had admired, such as *The Great Escape* and *Séance on a Wet Afternoon*. His first experience of Attenborough the director came when Kline was filming *The Big Chill* in Beaufort, South Carolina. The *Big Chill* like *Gandhi* was a Columbia movie and as a treat for the ensemble cast the company arranged a special New Year's Day screening of the movie for them. Kline's principal memory is of the fact that although the local cinema agreed to run the film they forgot to turn on the heating so the high-priced talent involved in his movie sat bundled up in coats and jackets watching *Gandhi*. But in spite of the cold he and the others were captivated by it and Kline had no hesitancy whatsoever when Attenborough approached him to play Donald Woods.

'I was in from the get go,' he says. 'I loved the story. It was unlike anything I had ever done and I wasn't worried about it not being a flashy part. I felt it was something I could really sink my teeth into. I knew it was going to be a study in subtlety and accuracy to get it right and I just wanted to be part of this movie in whatever way I could. I had been doing *Hamlet* on stage in New York when Dickie came over to see me. We spoke after the show and he gave me the script. I read it straightaway and when we spoke again the following morning I told him I loved it. It was not a great part but it was a great script and I wanted to be involved in telling this story, especially to Americans who knew little or nothing about apartheid at that time. The state of emergency in South Africa meant there was a press blackout and little or no information about what was going on was actually coming out. It seemed to me that this was the perfect way to tell the story, through a family that people could identify with and relate to. I knew it was not a flashy part, I was sort of a guide for the audience through this movie. In a way I was a bit like the camera.'

One of the things that Attenborough was most keen for Kline to do was to meet and get to know Donald Woods. Kline was equally keen because he knew

Kevin Kline in *Cry Freedom*

that as the focus of the movie he had to know what it felt like to 'be' Donald Woods. Happily, Kline and Woods got on famously and became fast friends, whiling away the time on set by playing complicated word games which kept them both amused for hours. The film was based on two books by Woods and he and his wife Wendy were involved right from the very beginning of shooting. It was a strange and novel experience for both of them and one which Donald Woods recalls in his own book *Filming with Attenborough*.

'Donald was slightly more involved than I was,' Wendy Woods remembers, 'but Dickie was very keen that we were both involved from the beginning. He wanted to know as much as possible about the South African situation so that he could make the best film he could. So he needed to know a lot, and quickly, but he is very good at doing that. He got John Briley, who was writing the script to consult with us all the time. I naïvely thought there would be a few little changes from his version and that would be the script. In the end there were 14 drafts, I've never seen such work. We went over to France where Dickie and Sheila have a house and we had these meetings every day where we would go over the script from beginning to end and there were always discussions and arguments. Make no mistake, these were strong arguments. Dickie would be there to referee, as it were, but there were occasions when there was blood on the floor. Jack had this view that he wanted Biko to be more like Gandhi – more passive – and we knew he wasn't, so that had to be worked out. I suppose there was a difficulty in tailoring the events to make the movie but that is something that you have to do. I realise now that once you are into that kind of thing you are constrained and you have to explain a lot, you can't make it for people who read the papers or go to the theatre and know what's going on. So all of those things had to be ironed out, which is why it took the 14 drafts.'

Donald Woods and Kevin Kline are not ever likely to pass for identical twins. But apart from getting used to a major movie star as her 'husband', Wendy also had to get used to seeing someone on screen pretending to be her. As well as hearing her own words in someone else's voice. 'The first time I was in the studio they were casting my part,' she says. 'There was this little set in the middle of this huge hangar-like place and we were standing in the shadows watching this actress. Someone said, "Action" and she just started to emote, which I found fascinating. It was doubly fascinating because those were my words coming out of her mouth. Jack had asked me for details of some of the things Donald and I had said to each other and I told him about the huge argument which we'd had about leaving South Africa, which became the beach scene in the movie. So he went away and put it in the script, which is why I was standing there listening to several actresses speaking my words. It was really weird but I got used to it.

'I was very aware of being invited into Dickie's world. Donald and I were standing there very much as outsiders and Dickie introduced us to Terry Clegg and David Tomblin and it was very much like this was his playground. I used to watch him standing on the set and absolutely loving it. I think he likes directing more than he likes anything else in the whole world, he gets totally taken up with it and all the emotions are going on in his face as he mouths the dialogue off-camera while the actors are playing their scenes. I often think he's like a little boy who has written to *Jim'll Fix It* to ask if he can direct a movie, the enjoyment he has is almost childlike. I used to think that it was because he was doing something he liked, he was directing a film. Then I watched him doing other things and if Sheila came up and asked his advice about a new colour scheme for the kitchen he would do that with the same enthusiasm. I find that enviable, I really do.'

Kevin Kline is equally admiring of his director's enthusiasm for his subject matter. He knew that both he and Attenborough had roughly the same ideas about the subject so he wasn't expecting to have to discuss things in great depth. Kline travelled to London where they were doing tests on some of the actors who were being considered for Biko before going on to Zimbabwe for a ten-day recce with Attenborough, Woods, and John Briley. There were long car journeys to remote locations and during conversations with Briley and Woods, Kline began to get some sense of the character, although he recalls that it wasn't done in the specific. There was lots of discussion about the generality of the

Robert Downey learned to play tennis left-handed in the style of Charlie Chaplin

Attenborough rehearses Robert Downey Jnr in *Chaplin*

Richard Attenborough offers advice to Robert Downey Jnr on *Chaplin*

Attenborough and Downey are hugely entertained by young Hugh Downer's stage performance as the boy Chaplin

Geraldine Chaplin and Robert Downey Jnr meet for the first time on the set of *Chaplin*

Attenborough, Downey and Diane Lane as Paulette Godard in *Chaplin*

Attenborough and Kevin Kline as Douglas Fairbanks in *Chaplin*

Attenborough and Diana Hawkins on *Shadowlands*

Alan Parker, Anthony Hopkins and Richard Attenborough share a joke on
Shadowlands

Attenborough and Debra Winger during shooting of the station scene in
Shadowlands

Attenborough discusses a scene with Anthony Hopkins on *Shadowlands*, their
fifth film together

Attenborough the actor in his latest movie role in *Miracle on 34th Street*

South African situation and he arrived at his characterisation almost by a process of osmosis.

'Dickie didn't talk about it a great deal,' he recalls. 'He knows that with actors it's almost as important to know when to leave them alone as it is to know what to say. Occasionally he would carry this to such an extreme that I used to have to beg him to rehearse sometimes. One of the joys about working with Dickie is that he is emotionally available, he's not shy about his feelings. When he would direct you he would be punctilious about not giving you a line reading. If the line wasn't coming out quite the way he wanted then he might say, "I think it's more . . . I don't want to give you a line reading but ...", and then he would just look at you and his face would contort into all these wild expressions. It was so effective that straight away you thought, "Ah, I see what you mean." He didn't need to give a line reading, just by the availability of his own emotional equipment as an actor himself he was able to communicate what he wanted quite effortlessly. The scene I remember most is the first one we shot where the security police come to my house and start to make all sorts of threats to me and my family. I had just finished doing *Hamlet* on stage of course and I remember Dickie saying, "Darling, we're right here, we're right here," and he was holding his hands at my forehead and at my chin to show me where the camera would be. It was like telling me that the scene should be intimate, that it shouldn't be too big, I shouldn't emote. That's the way he directs. Other than maybe reminding me of where the camera was, he trusts an actor's instinct.'

Like everyone else on the movie, Kevin Kline had a bodyguard. He has strong memories of standing in line for lunch and bumping into men with AK-47 machine-guns slung over their shoulders. Kline and Denzel Washington also had armed drivers who doubled as bodyguards for fear of attempts by white extremists to disrupt the film. Kline only found out after the film that there had in fact been an incursion and someone had got on to the set but it was kept quiet so that no one was too worried.

'I don't think Dickie's SAS bodyguards were too much of an encumbrance to him,' says Wendy Woods. 'They were very much in the background and when we were in the hotel they were very unobtrusive but I don't think he really wanted that protection. But he is very streetwise, that incident in the toilet with the two Afrikaners showed that. He loves showing off and I do enjoy watching him enjoying showing off. In fact when we were first discussing the script Dickie would act out scenes for us and I enjoyed them so much I used to pretend I didn't understand just to get him to do it again. But he can also be very secretive, he can play his cards very close to his chest. I think he likes people to think of him as not being perhaps as streetwise as he is but he is at his most fascinating when he gets into full flight. Donald and I watched him at work making deals in Los Angeles and he is very good at doing it. He told me one day, "I never fight about the things I know I'm going to succeed in getting anyway." So he does go round people and he is charming and it works. People like to be treated properly and he treats everyone very well, from the big stars to the carpenters and the electricians on the set. He likes people and he is nice to them. He knows what he is doing, he's well aware that if he treats people right he is more likely to get what he wants. It is manipulative in a way but it wouldn't come across the way it does if he was faking it. He is a genuinely nice man.

'He can also get angry. He did get angry at times with Donald and me and I was very taken aback. A lot of people can't handle their anger and they come out with all sorts of things but he would get red in the face and say he was angry because of this, this, and this and it was out in the open there and then. The next day it was gone and there was no lingering resentment. That's very rare, especially in an Englishman. It's the same with the crying business, he is not ashamed of his emotions. I think it's actually quite comforting to be around a man like that because with him the tears and the anger everything is there in the open. What you see is what you get and I like that. It's very nice to be with him because there is a lot of emotional exchange with him and that's very gratifying. It's certainly much more interesting than with people who are very reserved. It's what psychologists call an effective exchange of emotions rather than intellect and that's always much more interesting.'

Cry Freedom was again a film of set pieces. From the solemn splendour of Steve Biko's funeral to the awful carnage of the township massacres the film had a grandeur and sweep which made its strong political message easier to digest. Attenborough was at the centre of this whole operation, like a general with his army, and loyal lieutenants like Tomblin and Clegg would arrange for thousands of extras to be marshalled in and out as they were required. At times this forced a certain remoteness on the part of the director, who was frequently hundreds of yards away from the action. And for Kevin Kline, who was invariably in the thick of it, that remains his one regret about making *Cry Freedom*.

'We didn't always get to work as intimately as I would have liked,' he says. 'I remember a shot during the escape where I have to cross a bridge dressed as a priest. Dickie was out on a huge scaffold that had been built out in the middle of the river because that was the only way to get the shot and we were communicating by walkie-talkie. At one point I said, "Dickie, I'm thinking of putting my glasses on surreptitiously when I'm halfway across, I think it would be nice for Donald to be able to see where he is going for a change and then I could have them on when I meet the guy on the other side." And what I heard from the handset was Dickie saying: "Fine darling, that sounds very good. I'm not sure that we'll actually see it with this lens but you go ahead." My concern was matching continuity in close-up but because we were communicating by walkie-talkie it was not an intimate experience, I couldn't see those facial expressions I had become used to and that happened frequently because of the epic scale of the film. Dickie was always very concerned about the framing of the shot and I remember another scene with me and John Hargreaves who played the Australian journalist who helps me escape. We were looking at a map on the bonnet of a car and there is an army convoy in the background. Dickie always wanted to know how the background turned out. He might be told that birds flew across when we said such and such a line, or the convoy came in at such and such a point and I used to ask him jokingly if any of the acting had got

Opposite: Denzel Washington's Steve Biko and Kevin Kline's Donald Woods: a publicity shot for *Cry Freedom*

in the way of his background. It wasn't a hand-held documentary so of course he had to be concerned with the framing and the composition. But if the acting had been off Dickie wouldn't have used it no matter how good the convoy was.'

Cry Freedom is a rarity among Attenborough films in that the finished product is radically different from the shooting script. The movie was completely turned around once he got it into the editing suite. The editor on *Cry Freedom* was Lesley Walker who was succeeding an Attenborough favourite John Bloom. He had cut *Gandhi* but he had trained Lesley Walker so Attenborough felt he was in good hands. She remembers it as a very nervous experience because although they were filming in Zimbabwe the footage was being flown back to London where she was constructing a rough assembly on her own.

'I was very, very nervous about this,' she says looking back on the experience. 'I took my first few scenes out to Zimbabwe to let him see them privately to find out if I was on the right track. They didn't have a proper screening-room as such, it was just a hut lined with old egg boxes for sound-proofing. My intention was to go out and see it with him alone but when I got there he had invited everybody and I almost died. It was only 20 minutes of cut footage but it was 20 minutes which could have been totally wrong. I didn't know because I didn't have any kind of working relationship with him. Happily, he liked what I had done and from them on I could assemble very freely. I had a very free hand with the first assembly and after that it was just a question of going into the cutting-room and coming up with ideas and edits.'

There are a lot of directors who won't go near the cutting-room but Attenborough is not one of them. He knows by instinct what he wants once he gets over the editing desk. His sense of what is required may be more emotional than visual but it's that sense of passion that drives him and his movies. It was in the cutting-room with Lesley Walker that Attenborough and his editor realised that, as it stood, *Cry Freedom* wasn't working.

'The area which caused problems was Steve Biko's death,' she recalls. 'It wasn't originally as it was in the finished film, he died much earlier in the script and a lot of his appearances in the movie were in flashback. In essence he was originally supposed to have died in reel four but in the finished movie he died about halfway through and that came about in the cutting-room. Both Richard and I thought that the flashbacks were great but there is no getting away from the fact that the audience would know Biko had gone and the emotional content seemed to float out the door. So we solved that by playing Biko's courtroom scenes for real. I think it hit us both between the eyes at the same time. These scenes were all intended to be flashbacks during Donald's escape, they were never in the main film and emotionally that was a big letdown. You'd lost the man in reel four and you were then on a hiding to nothing.

'I think that demonstrates enormous flexibility on Richard's part and one you might not find in some directors. The script is always his bible but if something isn't working then he is definitely open to all suggestions. All of the story was coming through Donald and although it is in essence Donald's story that's not all that you're interested in at the start of the film. The courtroom scenes show what a fascinating man and charismatic leader Steve Biko was. By moving those scenes into the body of the film Donald's escape could then be slightly truncated because it had been lengthened by the flashback. This has the effect of pushing Donald forward more. Some critics said the film had two paces, the front half and the back half. I think that is accurate but I don't think it's a bad thing. I think the difference in pace works rather well. I certainly think it's a better way around the movie and it all came out of working closely with the director in the cutting-room.'

When it was released *Cry Freedom* was a disappointment at the American box office. The reviews were generally good and the film opened strongly in some selected cinemas but failed to build on that when it went on wider release. The general consensus was that it was a film ahead of its time. Within 18 months even the American public could not ignore apartheid and American cities saw the demonstrations outside South African embassies and government offices which had become commonplace in other countries. By then *Cry Freedom* had come and gone in box-office terms.

'Part of the problem I think is that black Americans are not Africans,' says Lesley Walker. 'At that time they had not quite cottoned on to what was happening in South Africa. I think if you had waited three more years, by which time black actors, black directors, and black issues were more of a force in Hollywood, then politically they would have been interested. At the time *Cry Freedom* was released, however, it was another world. South Africa was simply too far away for the American cinema-going public to be interested. I think, though, if it had come out say two years ago it would have done a lot better because the Americans have a better sense of what is going on in the world.'

Like Lesley Walker, everyone connected with *Cry Freedom* is inordinately proud of having made it and Kevin Kline for one is philosophical about its lack of commercial success. 'I would have no hesitation in working with Dickie, again any time, any place,' he says. 'But next time I'll pick my own people with high-powered rifles.'

Fighting for Charlie Chaplin

The question I am most often asked about Chaplin is: 'Why make a film about Charlie Chaplin?' For me the answer is quite simple. I love heroes and I have lots of heroes and one of my principal heroes for all sorts of reasons is Charlie Chaplin. I discovered him and fell in love with him when I was 11 and my father took me to London to see one of his films. We went to the National Gallery and then to see this man whom he called 'a genius' in *The Gold Rush*, which was being revived at the Pavilion Cinema in Piccadilly Circus, and I was entranced. I was absolutely shattered by him. It seemed extraordinary that a man could make you laugh and cry at the same time. I suppose if someone was to ask me why I wanted to become an actor or what it was that confirmed me in my wish to become an actor then I would have to say it was seeing *The Gold Rush* at that age.

The second reason was because I knew him and liked and admired him very much indeed. The first time we met was in a restaurant in the South of France in the Fifties. I was with Sheila and our children and there was a table in another part of the restaurant with another family party. At about six o'clock they got up to go and I realised it was Charlie Chaplin and his family. On the way out he came over to me. I just went scarlet – I might have been meeting Beethoven or Shakespeare. He said, 'How do you do? I have seen some of your work and admired it.' Of course I absolutely adored him from that moment on. No actor could resist such flattery. On the other occasions that we met I was terribly touched by his relationship with his last wife, Oona. She looked after him the whole time. If Oona went out of the room he would still keep talking to you but his eyes would constantly be on the door waiting for her to come back.

When my partner Diana Hawkins and I first decided to do the film I put the idea to Charlie's daughter Geraldine and she suggested I talk to her

135

A thoughtful moment for Attenborough on the set of *Chaplin*

mother. I wrote to Oona and she replied saying some very flattering things about *Gandhi* and offered me the screen rights to Charlie's autobiography. Her only condition was that there were to be no conditions. She didn't wish to have any influence on the screenplay or the casting. She said she wanted a film that was scrupulously honest and didn't hide anything. She said: 'You must make your view of Charlie, it must be your film. To make a hagiography, to be purely sycophantic, would be an insult to him.'

But even with all of this there was one overriding reason for making this film. My world is the movies. I've been doing it for more than 50 years, and it's the world that I inhabit, it's the world that I care about, it's the world where I find it possible to fill every minute of every day with total joy. And the man who is probably, if not certainly, as responsible as anyone else for creating what we know today as the movies is Charlie Chaplin. You can have arguments and debates about whether Buster Keaton or Harold Lloyd or Laurel and Hardy are greater comedians but nobody changed the movies as Charlie did. He pushed out the frontiers. He said movies are capable of almost anything and he in a way was responsible probably for turning them into the greatest communication medium of this century, as well as its art form.

I think to a certain extent that there may also have been a desire to rehabilitate him, or at least his reputation. When you ask someone today if Chaplin was funny they will invariably tell you Buster Keaton was funnier and I can't help thinking how silly those arguments are. I remember meeting two people in the same evening, one who thought Olivier's *Othello* was probably the greatest performance they'd ever seen and one who left after the first interval. How do you judge such a thing? What criteria do you apply? It's impossible. I don't think that all of his movies were wonderful – he himself certainly didn't think they were – but I think there are moments in almost every major movie that he has ever made of sheer unequivocal genius. I suppose you could put *Modern Times*, *City Lights*, and perhaps *The Great Dictator* ahead of others but I'm not sure – others might disagree with me. But then if you choose those what about *The Gold Rush*? It's impossible really. They are all part of a series of magical pieces of cinema entertainment, of genius clowning. He was unique in terms not only of performing but of creating and directing and producing and scoring and so on. If people nowadays find it easier to dismiss someone of Charlie's calibre then I don't think they understand or appreciate what he actually achieved and if that's the case then I really hope that perhaps this film might make them think again.

The great difficulty was in picking the moments to illustrate the genius of the man, whether it was the dance of the bread rolls in *The Gold Rush* or the taxi sequence in *City Lights* where the blind girl mistakes Charlie's drunken tramp for a millionaire. It was impossible really and largely arbitrary and I'm sure many people would say I made the wrong choices. The difficulty – no, not the difficulty – the concern in selecting them was of course that they should not be there purely in their own right. They had to contribute to a scene or they had to move the plot on, or they had to introduce another character, or whatever. Yes there are six, eight, 12, 20 wonderful moments of genius in Charlie's films but the actual selection was determined in some degree by the requirement of the overall plot. In addition, there was also the fact that at the end of the movie we show part of the compilation which was shown at the actual Oscar ceremony at which he was awarded – at the age of 83 – an honorary Oscar. Those clips selected themselves and the other ones we chose had to be selected in the light of that last sequence.

There was a major debate about whether or not we should use those original clips because we were well aware that we could be making a rod for our own back because of the tremendous strain they would place on the actor playing Charlie. Whoever we chose would have to be able to match up to what was in those clips. When Diana first wrote the actual outline she envisaged using the genuine material and I think she was absolutely right, no matter how far we may have veered away from that at one time or another. On the other hand, I think that we had to think carefully about the really sensational moments, for instance the moment in the cabin in *The Gold Rush* when Charlie is flaying about as the cabin tips over the edge of the cliff. Now, if you are going to attempt to reproduce that, you have to reproduce it exactly, which is well nigh impossible. Even the bread-rolls dance would have been a pale imitation if we had attempted to recreate it in its original context. I think once we decided to show the moments of genius, we had to show the moments that made him the most famous man in the world, the man who had made more people laugh than anyone had ever done before, then they had got to be the real thing. Therefore you decide that however tough that is, having accepted that as a prerequisite, you have got to then adjudge everything in the light of that decision.

Both Diana and I believed it would be sacrilege to attempt to mimic any of Chaplin's great movie performances so we had to find an actor who truly could look like the man himself. Another requirement was to find an actor with Charlie's amazing agility who could not only pull off the stunts Charlie used to do, but could also replicate his distinctive stance. If you ever saw Chaplin out of character he walked and stood very much like a marionette. Finally, we needed an actor who had a fine ear for accents. Anyone can walk along twiddling a cane but it takes a man of real talent to capture Charlie's changing Cockney accent which had a peculiarly pedantic edge to it. I am quite certain that in Robert Downey we found the perfect man for the role.

I first met Robert in my agent's office in Los Angeles. There was a knock on the door and this young man came in with hair sticking out in spikes with big black boots and rings in his ears – I'm not even sure he didn't have a ring in his nose. He was absolutely LA bratpack, there was no question of that whatsoever. All he did was to announce that he was going to play Chaplin, that he was the one actor who could play Chaplin and would I test him. I agreed. I can't say that I was totally convinced at that point. Obviously I would have preferred an English actor to have played a character who was born and bred in the East End of London as Charlie was but I couldn't find one. Ultimately we selected three English and four American actors. We went to America and, having decided on the seven, there was no doubt whatsoever

about Robert. He simply burst out of the screen. Not that he was any better than all the actors at turning their toes out, twiddling a cane with a bowler on their head – that's simple, you don't deserve an Equity ticket if you can't do that – but what was remarkable was that he provided the fire in the belly and the turmoil behind the eyes. This was vital because of all the words that should be selected as as far as Charlie is concerned the key one is the word 'passion'. He was passionate about everything that he did, whether it was his love affairs or whether it was his commitment to what he thought was the right way to behave in terms of the subject matter that he chose or whether it was the overriding passion of his work. Passion controlled everything. Once you accept that, a mass of other things fall into place and that's what Robert had. Robert had the ability to convey that driving, unqualified determination to achieve what he set out to achieve.

At that stage the film was still called *Charlie* – we changed it later to avoid confusion with the Cliff Robertson movie *Charly* – and it was being financed by Universal. The deal ultimately fell through and it has been suggested that this was because they were unhappy with the casting of Robert in the title role. That may be absolutely correct but I truthfully do not know. All I know was that having asked if they would agree to my casting him and their having said they would and having eventually, after a great deal of bargaining one way and another, agreed the terms of his contract at the last moment, they actually refused to sign it. They procrastinated for weeks and weeks. There was always some excuse, the lawyer was ill or somebody else was on holiday or the cat had eaten the contract. Anything, any reason other than actually signing. I felt strongly that it was improper to treat an actor in this way and finally I got to the point where I said either they signed Robert or they could call the picture off as far as I was concerned. They decided they would rather call the picture off. Now, whether they did that because of Robert, preferring a bigger name, whether it was because the budget was higher than they anticipated, whether the script wasn't what they thought it should be, or whether it was the distress caused by the costly failure of the very expensive *Havana*, which had been made at the same studio, I don't know. I genuinely still do not know their reasons but they, as we say, put the picture in turnaround, which gave me a year to raise the money from elsewhere and reimburse Universal for the money they had already invested in the picture.

I don't think it's quite true to say, as was rumoured at the time, that they wanted Dustin Hoffman. I think that they would have been very thrilled if there had been an actor of Dusty's skill and box-office appeal who could play Charlie. But the thing about *Chaplin* is that the film is not about an old man or even a middle-aged man, but about a young man. It is a film about young people. Charlie Chaplin, Mary Pickford and Doug Fairbanks took over Hollywood before they were 30. It's about a young man and sadly therefore Dusty, Robin Williams, Billy Crystal and other names who had been mentioned were all 15 years too old.

The picture was now in turnaround but Carolco – the independent production company behind films like *Terminator II* and the *Rambo* series –

got involved almost immediately even though they didn't actually execute their part of the deal for some considerable time. My agent Marti Baum said to me: 'We will go and see Mario Kassar. Mario has said right from the word go to me and, I happen to know, also to Tom Pollock at Universal – that if we ever needed backing one of the ambitions of his life was to make a film about Charlie Chaplin.' So Marti, Diana and I went to this extraordinary house full of a variety of valuable paintings with an enormous projection room which really went back to the heyday of Darryl Zanuck or Jack Warner. We talked about the film and I showed him Robert's test. He thought it was great. He said he was sure he could raise the money. He had a partner called Peter Hoffman who arranged all the business deals. We went to see him and he began by saying that he thought he would have major problems raising the foreign finance. In fact the opposite happened and we got the money from overseas in about 48 hours. I suppose that's indicative of the response to my films overall. Instead of the normal 60:40 in favour of America, we're about 70:30 in reverse. I usually take about 70 per cent overseas and 30 per cent in America. They got the promise of the money from abroad very quickly then had problems assembling their share of the investment. Although Mario said yes straight away in the end it took about six months before all the finance was in place. We went to see them in February and didn't get the green light until September.

This was most dreadful of all for Robert who was giving up other things while he was eating, breathing and talking Chaplin. Some of the sets were already built and we had to put security guards on them. The London street had to be kept up for months on end, the opening sequence of the East End had been built behind King's Cross station, and we had to keep all that together. There was even the possibility of legal action there because we were apparently violating some ancient statute about blocking the light of people living nearby. It was a cruel period simply because they never intimated it would take that long.

Mario is an extraordinary figure. He is a buccaneer who has made films like *Rambo* and *Terminator 2* but his overriding attribute is that he absolutely adores movies. He watches movies all day and every day and knows everything about them there is to know. There was only one real dispute I had with Mario and that was over the length of the movie. He left me totally free and only came on to the set twice. The casting was totally my decision except that he set down certain names, such as Tony Hopkins, Kevin Kline and Dan Aykroyd, that he would like to have. I have a very rare privilege engineered entirely by Marti Baum after *Gandhi* which is that I have what is called 'final cut'. This is not the normal Directors Guild of America final cut which allows you to go through a series of previews but ultimately the distributor has the final say. With me the distributor has to accept my cut and there is nothing they can change. Around the world I'm sure they probably do but legally I could have them. But my right of final cut does carry one prerequisite which is that the picture must not run more than 135 minutes. Either by conviction or by virtue of the contracts in this instance Carolco had signed all around the

Diana Hawkins, Terry Clegg and Attenborough on location for *Chaplin*

world, the picture had to be no longer than 135 minutes. Mario demanded that pound of flesh, as it were.

I understand the principle. If you don't make *Terminator 2* and you make movies that principally do their business on Friday, Saturday and Sunday then the exhibitor must have the ability to get two performances in per night. I understand that principle but I think that to follow it slavishly is a grave error. Look at *Schindler's List* or *Dances With Wolves*, they both run to three hours plus and have taken enormous amounts of money. Nevertheless, Mario stood firm.

It was also Mario's insistence that the scenes in Switzerland be included. With Bill Goldman we arrived at a very precise construction that came in large measure from our conviction that Charlie's life was incredibly integrated; between youth and experience and the impact of all he had suffered. You could not leave anything out or else the whole structure collapsed. We had a very, very integrated shape for the movie. The sad thing is that I made a mistake. I got the timing wrong and it was entirely my fault. Instead of coming out at 135 minutes the picture ended up at 147 minutes and because of its final construction there wasn't a single section you could lift out in isolation. So instead of deciding not to show his youth, or deciding to take out his political convictions, for instance, we had to go through the movie and take out tiny little bits. You couldn't release one of these director's cuts of *Chaplin* which are so fashionable these days because it would mean redubbing the whole picture. It wouldn't be just a case of putting this or that section back; there were hundreds of tiny little cuts which the editor Anne Coates and I made and I have to say it broke our hearts. I think that at the end of the day – and this is not being disloyal to Mario because he supported me absolutely down the line as nobody else would have done – the circumstances which resulted in a running time of 135 minutes instead of 147 minutes inevitably damaged the picture significantly.

The one other important element in the post-production of *Chaplin* was the music. I had wanted to work with John Barry again for a long time but our schedules had never actually permitted it. I think Bryan Forbes and I gave John almost his first job in movies when he wrote some of the music for a film we made called *The L-Shaped Room*. He then did the full score for *Séance on a Wet Afternoon*. He's a brilliant composer by any standard and I think he has an extraordinary talent, being able to capture essentials not merely of a movie as a whole but of a particular scene. He is also able then to find a way of using that piece of music, that fundamental theme, in all sorts of forms so that by the time he reiterates it it's like hearing a melody line. He has a wonderful ability to create a very simple melodic line which can be very touching without ever being mawkish, and that was very important on *Chaplin*. I think his score has huge sentiment without being slushy at all, he's a very, very clever composer.

It was also while we were involved in the post-production and putting the finishing touches to *Chaplin* that I decided to return to acting. It was all because of Steven Spielberg, there is no question about that. This was the third time he had asked me to act for him and I had never been able to but this time he put it the other way round. He said, 'Look I know that you're editing and dubbing and recording the music for *Chaplin*. You tell me when you've got to be in England and we will schedule the movie so that you only have to be in Los Angeles or Hawaii between those periods.' The film was of course *Jurassic Park*. My actor's ego was flattered to a point where I simply couldn't say no. I loved the experience but I was frightened to death prior to my first day. When I told Robert Downey that I was so panicked that I could scarcely breathe he roared with laughter. 'Serves you right,' he said. 'Now you know what it's like.' I hadn't done it for a long time – it had been almost 15 years since I did *The Human Factor* for Otto Preminger – and I had a lot of dialogue on the first day. I was so nervous I didn't sleep a wink the night before. When I went on the set I hoped not too many people guessed the extent to which my stomach was in knots with nerves, I just prayed I would be able to get through the lines without them having to bring out the idiot boards.

When it was released *Chaplin* was not a great commercial success by any means. Although it did well in the UK and various other parts of the world it was not exceptional; after all, it's not *Terminator II*. It was also savaged by the majority of British critics, which I am still puzzled about – I don't understand that at all. I don't mind if people don't like the film and criticise the movie, but what I can't accept are people using their position as critics to make personal attacks either on myself or Charlie. I have one great concern in terms of the London critics – and what is strange is that it has been confined to the London critics. If you look at some of the reviews received in Birmingham, Manchester, or Glasgow, they were totally different. You would not have thought they were watching the same movie. In America we had two rough reviews but the rest were enthusiastic. I think in a strange way, particularly in London, there is a tendency of denigrating our national heroes. There is this contemporary fashion to denounce Charlie Chaplin as unfunny, which is, of course, absolute nonsense. For more than three decades Chaplin was the most popular comic performer in the world and one of the few truly global movie stars. To dismiss him simply as unfunny just reveals the stupidity of 'hose who make such absurd statements.

Chaplin Reborn

From the moment he burst in on Richard Attenborough in Marti Baum's office there was no doubt in Robert Downey Jnr's mind that he would play Chaplin. For the young American it was the part he was born to play and he would let nothing come between him and Charlie. Even when the film was put into turnaround Downey was never in any doubt that it would go ahead and that he would ultimately star in it. But why was the role so important?

'For the opportunity,' he says simply. 'He was a great artist. He was the first performer to combine being an entertainer with being a social commentator and critic as well. There have been only a handful of entertainers in the world – and I include Sir Richard Attenborough among them – who have been able to hold a mirror up to nature. That's what was so important about this man and that was our goal. I believe that goal was achieved. There has been so much misinformation spread about Charlie that here was a golden opportunity to set the record straight. Of course the man had his imperfections – and we did not gloss over his liking for young women – but he was also a man with terrific integrity, which is a rare quality in Hollywood.'

A tow-headed, amiable young man, Downey had previously appeared in movies like *Less Than Zero*, *Air America* and *Soapdish*. The son of the respected independent film maker Robert Downey, he had made his screen début at the tender age of five playing a puppy in one of his father's films. Larger roles followed and by the time he was being considered by Attenborough Downey was a veteran of some 19 films. When he was cast in *Chaplin* he was seen as a young man on the brink of breaking out of the generic Los Angeles bratpack. His performance in the film and his subsequent Best Actor Oscar nomination confirmed his status as one of Hollywood's heirs apparent. Downey was well aware of the lengths that Attenborough had gone to in order to make sure he got the part; there are few actors who have had their directors voluntarily put the film into turnaround because of the way the actor was being treated by the studio. But in the midst of the row over his casting Downey had one important ally even if he did not yet know it.

Geraldine Chaplin is the oldest of Chaplin's eight children with Oona O'Neil and she was involved in the project from a very early stage. When her mother gave Attenborough the go-ahead for the film one of his first actions was to offer Geraldine the part of her own grandmother. Charlie's mother, Hannah, spent her life in and out of asylums and workhouses while her sons were growing up. Geraldine jumped at the role when it was offered to her.

'My father talked about Hannah a lot, and with great affection,' she explains. 'He adored her, he never said she was insane but he would tell funny stories about her and we could see that she was. I was always tempted to be in the film though because it was going to be a major motion picture with Sir Richard directing and it was such a wonderful part. I didn't realise though that it would be so painful until I saw Hannah on the screen. It was a great part but a real blow to see her like that.'

But it was something else she had seen which convinced Geraldine Chaplin that her father's memory would be treated with respect and with integrity. After she had agreed to play Hannah, the director took her to a small theatre in Los Angeles and showed her one of the scenes which had already been shot with Downey. When the lights came up after a quarter of an hour of footage Geraldine was sitting completely still. Then after what seemed to Attenborough to be a very long silence she turned round and said, 'I have to tell you, I had never, ever dreamed that anybody could convince me that they were daddy. But that young man WAS Daddy!'

No one was more relieved than Robert Downey Jnr when Attenborough relayed her reaction. He had dedicated himself to becoming Charlie Chaplin. He spent a year with a mime expert, changing his posture so that he held himself like Chaplin. He read everything about Chaplin he could lay his hands on, he watched all of his films again and again, and he pored over every newsreel and documentary that he could find in order to perfectly duplicate Chaplin's mannerisms. He even learned to play tennis left-handed as Charlie did, he spent days walking the back streets of London where Charlie grew up, and at the Museum of the Moving Image in London he persuaded staff to allow him to try on one of their most prized exhibits, Chaplin's *Little Tramp* suit and boots. Apart from the vicarious thrill of wearing Chaplin's clothes the actor also treasured a long-forgotten cigar stub that he discovered in one of the pockets. And all of this for a part he didn't know he would definitely play in a movie which might never actually get made.

In the period when they were both waiting to find out if the film would actually get a green light from Universal and subsequently Carolco, a strong bond grew between Downey and his director, who was acutely aware of the pressure on his star. Richard Attenborough has been called a great many things in his long career but Downey added a new description. 'Sir Richard was brilliant, he couldn't have been more helpful. I was like a pregnant woman

Opposite: Kevin Kline in swashbuckling mood with Robert Downey Jnr's Charlie Chaplin and Maria Pitillo's Mary Pickford

going through a particularly difficult labour and Sir Richard was the dedicated midwife. I felt he would never ask me to do things he couldn't help me through, he would go through every moment with me. I would ring him up in the middle of the night because I couldn't sleep for worrying about some small detail of Charlie's life, and he never seemed to mind. He might suggest that it could wait until morning but he never minded being called. He also had the knack of helping me in exactly the way that I wanted. There's a scene in the movie in which Charlie watches footage of The Great War. It must have been an incredibly distressing experience for him because he was watching his fellow countrymen die in the trenches at a time when he was feeling guilty about making movies in Hollywood. All I knew about war was seeing American newsreels from Vietnam, yet Sir Richard was able to talk me through this and let me know exactly the way Chaplin would have felt at seeing this devastating footage.'

Robert Downey Jnr knows that part of the reason that *Chaplin* fell through originally at Universal was that, for one reason or another, the studio did not have enough faith in him in the title role. Richard Attenborough did and that faith was the bedrock on which the remarkably strong link between the director and his star was founded. 'I feel my performance in this film had a lot to do with a lot of other people but primarily with Sir Richard. There were a lot of things that I simply didn't know before we started and I think I'm a very different person from the one I was before, and part of that has to do with our relationship. When someone who has been making films twice as long as I've been sucking air takes time to really give me so much of his experience and knowledge, that's really important. He never changed his mind when the studio lacked faith in me. He really was my champion and I was prepared to do whatever I had to do for him.'

Although the public perception is of a man who directs epics, Attenborough's reputation as an actor's director is well known in Hollywood and borne out by the quality of the cast assembled to support Downey in *Chaplin*. As well as Geraldine Chaplin, the cast included Anthony Hopkins, James Woods, Dan Aykroyd, Kevin Kline, Marisa Tomei, Penelope Anne Miller and Diane Lane. Aykroyd was so keen to work with Attenborough and to play fellow Canadian Mack Sennet that he rearranged his other commitments, enabling him to do all his scenes in a single week. James Woods went one better. Apart from agreeing to play a character he found morally repellent – the sleazy attorney who prosecuted Chaplin in his notorious paternity suit – Woods also agreed to shoot his courtroom sequence on his only free Saturday in months. And *Chaplin* also provided the chance for Attenborough to be reunited with one of his *Cry Freedom* stars when Kevin Kline agreed to play a supporting part as Charlie's great pal, swashbuckling star Douglas Fairbanks.

'Ordinarily, playing a cameo holds no great appeal to me,' explains Kline. 'But, as I told Dickie: "Whatever!" Also, Chaplin was a great inspiration to me when I discovered him halfway through my college career. There was a Chaplin Festival, I went along and suddenly a whole world opened up for me, it was just incredible. The only hesitancy was a scheduling problem. My wife was due to have our first child the week before he wanted me and I told him I couldn't just up and leave her. So he juggled the shooting schedule around so that I could actually have about five weeks with the baby before I had to take off for location and in fact in the end we all went together.'

Like Fairbanks, Kevin Kline made an early impression in Hollywood as a swashbuckler, in his case it was in *The Pirates of Penzance*, the big-screen version of the Gilbert and Sullivan light opera. Kline had reprised his stage role and Hollywood was eating out of his hand. His athleticism, his natural good looks and his ready wit had scripts piling up behind his door. Kline, however, resisted the temptation and refused to be typecast, choosing instead to vary his work with films like *Sophie's Choice*, *The Big Chill* and his Oscar-winning performance in *A Fish Called Wanda*.

'I had been asked numerous times to play Errol Flynn or John Gilbert but I always turned them down because I didn't really want to play another actor, it can end up like impersonation rather than acting. But when Dickie asked me to do Fairbanks I agreed because I thought that most people don't really know what he ever sounded like since he was known mostly from his silent movies. I don't look much like him and I'm built completely different so there was no point in doing a slavish impersonation. That was a pretty quick discussion when

The Three Musketeers: Marti Baum, Diana Hawkins and Richard Attenborough on the first day of Californian location shooting for *Chaplin*

we decided to try to capture the flavour of the man without actually trying to mimic him.'

Kline was, however, a little disappointed not to be able to impersonate Fairbanks's legendary athletic prowess. There are two moments of vintage Fairbanks in *Chaplin*: the first is when the action star swings down from a castle rampart on a rope to welcome Charlie to a party, the second is when Fairbanks turns the old Hollywoodland sign into an impromptu gym apparatus while he and Chaplin ponder their future.

'The first shot I did in the movie was swinging down on the rope and I said to Dickie: "Come on, let me do one." He said: "Absolutely not. If it was the last day of shooting I would consider it but this is the first day and I need you for the next eight days." Again on the Hollywood sign I said: "I can climb that." But the reply came back again. "Absolutely not!" In fact I did get to do some of my own climbing, though they had a stuntman there for the tricky stuff. And he did let me ride a horse and climb a tree – a scene which was cut from the movie, incidentally – and I got to fence with a sword, so he didn't take away all my toys.'

Having already worked with Attenborough on the highly political *Cry Freedom*, Kevin Kline was mildly but pleasantly surprised to discover that no matter what the subject is, an Attenborough movie is a labour of love. 'It was very interesting to do *Chaplin* after seeing the passion and commitment that went into getting *Cry Freedom* going. With *Chaplin* I came along about halfway into the shooting and my stuff was pretty light really. It was the nature of the character more than anything, it was kind of fun and bouncy and there was none of the kind of drama or political or social driving force to get it done. There was no noble cause behind *Chaplin* but there was definitely the same energy. And Dickie is not lackadaisical, there is a wonderful energy when he works which is very attractive and very infectious.

'Apart from his directorial style, he is just great fun to be around. You also know that there is this instinctive love for film. Dickie is also not ashamed of feeling and as a man that's nice to be around. I know he gets lampooned for it but he has a great sense of humour about himself and I have seen him wind himself up.'

Chaplin also brought Attenborough together once more with Oscar-winning screenwriter William Goldman, who had written *A Bridge Too Far* and *Magic*. Goldman was brought on by Mario Kassar as a 'script doctor', an established writer who is hired to punch up an existing script. Goldman is one of Hollywood's finest. His healing hands have worked their magic on films like *Twins* and *Indecent Proposal*. Unusually for a script doctor, Goldman ended up with a screen credit along with Bryan Forbes and William Boyd. However, he concedes that he is as mystified as anyone by that, citing the vagaries of the Writers' Guild's arbitration process.

For Goldman there was one major flaw in *Chaplin*. 'Movies don't cover time well and the things that moved Dickie most were the events that made up the whole sweep of this man's life,' he says. 'You could have made a whole movie out of the Dickensian childhood which ended with the discovery of the Little

Richard and Sheila Attenborough at the Royal Film Performance, 1992

Tramp. You could make a whole movie starting with Chaplin coming to America and ending with the international fame. You could make a whole movie out of the paternity case. You could make a whole movie out of his exile in Switzerland, whatever.

'What Dickie was most moved by was that incredibly impoverished Dickensian childhood and the terribly emotional time when Chaplin is in his eighties and gets an honorary Oscar. The problem with that is that if you want to do 75 years in a man's life you not only have to get involved with make-up – sometimes Downey was working 20 hours a day and going crazy – but things get very clunky. People say things they don't really say. They'll say: "Ah Dickie, it's good to see you here in London where I haven't been for 11 years since my wife died of cancer." People don't say that sort of thing but you have to make sure the audience gets the information about where I am, why my wife isn't there, and how much time has passed since I was there last.'

Goldman's solution to 'de-clunking' the movie was to introduce the scenes in Switzerland with Anthony Hopkins's character. He plays an editor jogging the memory of the now elderly Charlie as they go through the manuscript of his autobiography. Goldman never intended these scenes to be expository, although that is, in fact, how they turned out. 'These scenes were supposed to deal with material we had already seen and a put a new slant on it,' he explains. 'They became expository because there was no other way of handling the mass of material. I think *Chaplin* is a splendid-looking movie and Downey is absolutely wonderful but I think ultimately the reason the film did not work is that it is so hard to cover that span of years. It just is. I had read the book and my impulse would have been simply to tell the story of the childhood. I would have done what we did with *All the President's Men*, which was essentially to end on their screw-up because the audience knew that Woodward and Bernstein became famous. I would have tried to end the movie at the moment where Chaplin discovers the Little Tramp but that is not the movie that Dickie wanted to do.'

Among the most effective scenes in the movie are those set in 'Old Hollywood' where Chaplin, Fairbanks and Pickford reigned supreme in their heyday. Certainly for Geraldine Chaplin they brought the memories flooding back. When she walked on to the set which recreated Chaplin's old studio – now the headquarters of A&M Records on LaBrea Avenue just off Sunset Boulevard in Los Angeles – it was like turning back the clock. 'I was about five or six the last time I was there and I didn't remember that I remembered it,' she recalled. 'But when I came on to that set I suddenly recognised every door without actually consciously knowing it.'

Her first meeting with Downey in character produced a similarly unsettling reaction. 'I don't think that any actor could do what Robert did,' she says. 'It was as if my father came down from heaven and inhabited him and possessed him for the length of the movie. It was just so shocking, he's extraordinary. It's either as if my father was there, or else Robert is his reincarnation. He is so gorgeous, which is appropriate because my father was a beautiful man too. Robert does the Little Tramp perfectly and he seems to capture the essence of my father. He's heartbreaking and he has my father's sense of melancholy. The first time I met him as the Little Tramp I hugged him and he hugged me, and there I was with my father as a young man in my arms. We had quite a Freudian moment there,' she admits.

For Robert Downey Jnr there were no Freudian moments, just the realisation of the responsibility which he would carry on his shoulders. A responsibility, he wryly concedes, that his friends never tired of reminding him about. 'There were times when I thought: "Oh God, I'll never be able to show my face on set again. I don't know what I'm doing and everyone is going to find out." Having the chance to play someone like Chaplin was to experience everything from feeling honoured, to waking up sweating, convinced I was an absolute sham. I went through a whole host of emotions in taking this role from humility and frustration to feeling like I've really found myself. It has sent me off in all different directions – I feel reborn.'

But it could all have been very different. The story of *Chaplin* is a story of 'what if'. What if Carolco had said no? What if those elaborate sets had had to be left in storage? What if another part which was equally good had come along? Robert Downey Jnr knows the answers to all of these questions. 'Even if this movie had never gone ahead,' he says thoughtfully, 'knowing that if it had been done it would have been done with me, would have been reward enough.'

Into the Shadowlands

At the outset I would have to be honest and say I did not find *Shadowlands*, it found me. Nine times out of ten I have always chosen to originate my own material, whether it is *Chaplin, Cry Freedom,* or *Gandhi* or whatever, but with *Shadowlands* I cannot take any credit whatsoever. As most people know, it started as a TV play and then it was a phenomenal success in the West End and then on Broadway. It was all set up and created by the man who jointly produced the film with me, Brian Eastman, with Bill Nicholson writing the script from his original play.

I was in Hawaii filming *Jurassic Park* when Diana first read it; Brian having sent it to me. When I came back from Hawaii almost the first thing she said was: 'Dick, I've got a script that you've got to read. It's the best piece of writing for the screen I have read.' Of course when I read Bill's words it didn't seem to have originated as a piece of theatre at all. It was not only a beautifully conceived piece of work as far as the cinema was concerned but it had dialogue of a calibre and indeed, dare one say, an intellect which was remarkable. In fact it was as good a screenplay of a love story as I had ever read. It's also about two people of great interest, of substance – I'm reluctant to use the word intellect since I've always found that tends to put audiences off – but of substance. They were a man in his fifties and a woman in her late thirties to early forties. Jack Lewis and Joy Gresham came from different sides of the world with totally different attitudes and values and conducts of behaviour. The imagery of C.S. Lewis as this intellectual figure protected and cosseted by the atmosphere of academia – an atmosphere much more than would be found in any ordinary university – suddenly faced with the sudden invasion of this brash, outspoken, untraditional, Jewish divorcee from New York was like the devil coming into the cathedral. It created all sorts of sparks. Joy Gresham was a feisty lady and I know because I come from a not dissimilar background. My mother was not quite a suffragette but she invaded the cloistered sanctity of academe at my father's university. She was feisty and she was outspoken about women's rights and other things that she wanted to sound off about, exactly the same as Joy.

I knew that casting a film like *Shadowlands* would be of paramount importance. It is a two-hander and I perhaps ought to have played the two hands a little more cautiously than I did, but I was so certain. I was not all that familiar with Lewis's work. I had read *The Screwtape Letters*, of course, and from them I had an image of C.S. Lewis as Jeremy Irons, as an essentially ascetic character. But of course he's a second-row rugby forward. He's a butcher with great huge shoulders, a thick neck, and not ascetic-looking at all. I knew then that Tony Hopkins was just potentially the most wonderful casting. I got back from Hawaii on a Thursday night and read the script on the Friday evening while we were recording music for *Chaplin* at The Beatles studio on Abbey Road. I had been talking to Tony on the phone and I remembered him saying, because he loves music, that he would like to be around when we were doing some of it. He was due in the studio the following day, the Saturday, so I took the script with me.

Tony came in just before lunch and stayed for about an hour-and-a-half and before he left, wicked devil that I am, I gave him the script. I said, 'Tony, I've got a script here that came in. You might be interested to look at it?' Tony said he didn't want to read anything just at the moment but I persisted and he took the script. I got home I suppose around eight and there was a message to say would I phone Tony, so I did. I said: 'Hi Tony, it's Dick . . . ' and there was silence. So I said: 'Hello? Tony . . . ' Then there was this Welsh voice. 'You bloody devil,' he said. 'You devil, you knew exactly what you were doing, didn't you? I had to put that script down three times in order to get through it and the last time I had to go out and walk up and down outside the house. It's the most emotionally disturbing piece of writing I think I have ever read. What are you going to do with it?' I said I didn't know yet since I'd only read it the night before, but would he like to play Lewis? 'Like to?' he said. 'I'll kill any actor who came between me and this part.' And so we agreed to do it and by the following Tuesday evening, which was ten in the morning Los Angeles time, Brian and I had a verbal distribution agreement. I have never in my life had a film come together so easily.

Sadly, however, there wasn't a penny of British money in the film and that makes me thoroughly miserable. I used an entirely British crew and, with the exceptions of Debra Winger and Joey Mazzello, the cast is entirely British. There really ought to have been British money in this film because it made money all over the world and it could have brought millions of dollars back to the UK.

So with Tony agreeing to play C.S. Lewis there of course then arose the question of who should play Joy Gresham. I had one or two thoughts, one of which was definitely Debra Winger. One of the problems I think with the movie is that if it became sentimental as against a subject imbued with sentiment it would be really mawkish towards the end. Practically every actress in a certain age group wanted the part but I felt very strongly that apart from ability – and I met some quite superb actresses – you really needed someone who has an element of abrasiveness. Debra, of course, has a somewhat daunting reputation for being a difficult lady so I knew I would have to deal with that because I couldn't go to Tony with a problem before we had even started. I gathered that she had heard that I got the script, I also gathered that this was a part she said she desperately wanted to play. So I decided the thing to do was to level with her and I laid out all of my concerns.

Almost immediately she said she knew that she had been bloody stupid and got herself into some ridiculous positions because of people feeling she was difficult to deal with. She admitted that on one occasion she had been just plain obstreperous but on virtually all the other occasions it had been because she was unhappy with the work. She felt that it wasn't being tackled as seriously or as thoroughly as it ought to be and she couldn't bear that. 'I lose all sense of proportion,' she told me. 'But it's the work that matters, it's my life.' I told her that was absolutely fine with me. If she felt she had to stamp around and get shirty in order to wind herself up to a point where she was able to create particular emotions, then I wouldn't have a problem with that providing she came up with the goods. But, I warned her, 'I can't be bothered with all of that if you don't deliver, but if you can then that's fine. However, it has to be within reason and you have to consider the other people on the floor, particularly in this case your leading man.' The upshot was that she told me she would give anything to play the part and offered an absolute assurance that there would be no problems. Once, I think there was what you might call a spat which came out of a very emotional scene, but as far as her professionalism is concerned my admiration is unqualified. She was correct in everything she said, she didn't fuss about her trailer or any of that ludicrous star nonsense. She was always on time, she knew her words backwards, and she had always done the preparation for a particular sequence. She had her own thoughts about how she wanted to play it but equally she was never dogmatic. If Tony or I had other ideas then we debated them through. And she always ultimately allowed me to have my way. She was marvellous.

Having cast the two leading roles, there was another difficulty. It seemed to me that we would have enormous problems shooting this picture in terms of the variety of image which was available. Latterly, Joy was in bed or in a chair and therefore you couldn't move her around, so I realised I would have no alternative but to cross-cut. But it seemed that it might be quite interesting to shoot the film on the widest possible ratio and then as the two characters gradually got to know each other hold them more and more within the same set-up. We pulled the focus when I wanted the attention to go to either character as if it was a cut. By using Panavision we could shoot a scene such as the one where he goes up to London and visits her apartment almost in one set-up. I think there are only about three actual cuts altogether in that sequence and that also applied to the sequences where Jack is visiting Joy in hospital. I'd never seen focus used in quite that way before, or indeed to that extent. It was quite an innovative style in a way but I think it was worth it because it worked not merely as an integral part of those particular scenes but ultimately in terms of the wider emotional impact of the film.

I think a lot of my confidence came from working with a new cameraman, Roger Pratt. I found a remarkable empathy with him. We both come from Leicester and I suppose in a ludicrous way it set us off on a sort of intimacy. The fact that a lot of my closest friends had been wanting me to work with him meant that there was an imperative in what we were undertaking. But he's no pushover. If Roger doesn't think what you're doing is what you ought to be doing then you'll know. It may be ten minutes before you actually know because he doesn't exactly come out with guns blazing. Equally, anything that I suggested which was out of the ordinary, such as this idea, he jumped at and what was immensely comforting was that he felt confident that we had the focus puller to do it. Pulling focus is an immensely skilful job because actors change their timing between takes, as they should – not basically but in nuance – and if that focus throw is either just ahead or just behind that moment then the shot is ruined. Simon Hume did an extraordinary job, and so did camera operator Mike Roberts. I now consider myself fortunate to have worked with five great, great camera operators: Ronnie Taylor who did *Gandhi* and started with me on *Oh! What A Lovely War*, Peter Macdonald who not only was a sensational operator but did a lot of second-unit work on *Cry Freedom*, Tom Priestley who did *Chorus Line*, Eddie Collins on *Cry Freedom* and now lastly on *Shadowlands* probably the doyen, Mike Roberts. I don't think there was a single shot when Mike said: 'Didn't quite get it, can we go again?'

There are a number of people who have said that *Shadowlands* is the sort of film I ought to have been making for ages. In particular Ann Skinner, who was my very first continuity girl. There's a sort of myth in a way or at least it's a misunderstanding about the movies I make. I don't yearn for hundreds of thousands of people on the screen, I really don't. It so happens that the subjects that I have been fascinated by have been set against very considerable backgrounds of panoramic and epic scale. I quite enjoy putting all those people together but Terry Clegg and David Tomblin are much better at it than I and although I get the credit at the end of the day the credit belongs to Tomblin in large measure. The concept is mine but in those big movies the day-to-day execution was always David's. What I so enjoyed about *Shadowlands* was that there was an immediacy about it. Once I went on to the floor there weren't 35,000 people to organise. I was straight on to what I love doing most. There's nothing between me and the actors and nothing can get in the way or impinge upon the concentration I wished to make as far as the performances are concerned. It's a tremendously demanding situation for your actors in those other films, of course, because when you have got 35,000 people in the shot your principals have got to perform within that context. You don't have a great deal of freedom. Sometimes I would have to say, 'Sorry Ben you can't go again because 35,000 people have to go home', and that is a major constraint which simply didn't apply to *Shadowlands*.

Working with Debra Winger was doubly pleasing, not just because she is a great actress, but because the critics, some critics at least, love to attack

Richard Attenborough on *Shadowlands* with Director of Photography Roger Pratt (sitting) and 'the doyen of camera operators' Mike Roberts

Richard Attenborough frames a shot with Joey Mazzello in *Shadowlands*

me for being a misogynist in my movies. I didn't set out to do a movie with a strong female role in it to deliberately dispel that notion but it would be nice if *Shadowlands* did because it is such a load of balls, to coin a phrase. I also carry the label and the load, as far as some critics are concerned, of only making epic pictures and indulging in great *Ben Hur* type crowd scenes. In fact, as I have said, I do quite enjoy all of that but that is not the principal attraction for me. The attraction for me, even in the so-called epic pictures, is the characters in the foreground. All that is different with *Shadowlands* is that the background takes a very much less significant part in the conception in that the background is Oxford University. As far as I'm concerned, *Shadowlands* isn't really a great change because what I have always adored in movies, or indeed in theatre in the days when I was in theatre, is working with actors. That's the way I tell my stories, that's the way I convey what I want to say, through the actors not through pyrotechnics. In this film we have two phenomenally wonderful, three-dimensional, live, flesh-and-blood characters and their relationship is both fascinating and revealing. They don't start out in reel one and end up exactly the same in reel 12. Over the period of time in the movie they really change and develop. Tragically for one of them, of course, but it is a wonderfully moving story nonetheless.

Joey Mazzello, who plays Debra's screen son, Douglas, had to cope with some of the most emotional scenes in the film. I first encountered him during the shooting of *Jurassic Park* in which he played my grandson. I must admit that he didn't need a great deal of direction. He's an absolute gem and Tony and Debra and I hate him. We hate him with a loathing that you cannot begin to understand because at the age of nine he knows as much about acting as Tony and Debra and I have been trying to learn for goodness knows how many years. What's marvellous about Joey is that he is a pro. He's blessed with miraculous parents and he deals with the ridiculous business of fooling around in front of a camera wonderfully. Away from all of that he is a normal boy leading a normal life but the second he comes on to the floor you can talk to him exactly as you would talk to Tony or Debra. He works as a professional and he talks about scenes and what you want from him in them. For the scene where Douglas and Jack break down together in the attic after Joy's death we had to have four different angles. Every single time that we did it we watched those tears appear in his eyes and they were utterly real on each occasion because Joey understands that acting is believing. It's not pretending, it's not charades. It's being true to the material.

All actors have different approaches to the material. Debra will research to the point where she knows more about Joy Gresham than anyone else alive – she could recite Joy's poetry from memory – and it all goes into her head and she then uses it as required, but it tends to support her performance rather than dominate it. Tony will read a biography, perhaps two, and nothing else because he believes that what he has to convey is in the screenplay and anything which doesn't illuminate that screenplay is baggage. He may read the script 100 times, 150 times, and by the time he comes on to the floor he knows it absolutely backwards and he improvises. He doesn't like too much rehearsal and he will improvise right up to the first take when of course he is word perfect. There was a moment in fact when we thought Joey had dried up and someone said, 'Joey, your next line is so and so,'and Joey replied, 'I know my line, I haven't dried, it's just that Mr Hopkins hasn't said his line properly.' Tony has this extraordinary ability to make you believe when you hear him that it is the very first time he has ever said that line. It is an incredible gift.

I've directed Tony in five films now and he was more relaxed, more at ease on *Shadowlands*, in fact easier to direct than in any other film. He has always been an incredibly good actor. What has changed in Tony's life is that he lived in the shadow of Burton in Wales and in the shadow of Olivier at the National Theatre. That, I think, was the cause of the dreadful alcohol period from which, with phenomenal courage and strength of will, he ultimately emerged to take his rightful place. The profession gave him an Oscar, the country gave him a knighthood and Tony was no longer the inhibited introspective. He is still, to an extent, introspective and shy but the confidence he got from those two events and the success of *Howards End* and *The Remains of the Day* has convinced him that nothing is beyond his reach. At the time when we made *Magic* together he could no more have played Jack Lewis than flown to the moon. He was terrified. He couldn't play the love scenes with Ann- Margret. Now he has all this wonderful confidence and he can stand emotionally naked in front of us.

If you ask me, then I will answer the question. I think *Shadowlands* is the best piece of work Tony has ever done in his life. And I think if you talk about actors such as Emil Jannings, Paul Muni, Edward G. Robinson, Spencer Tracy, or Robert De Niro, at the end of that list for the 1980s and 1990s you will have to add Tony's performance in *Shadowlands*, I think he is simply miraculous, the actor of his generation.

A number of people have been kind enough to say that *Shadowlands* is my best film, but I have no intention of resting on whatever laurels I may or may not have. I absolutely adore making movies. My great sadness is that I only started to direct in 1969 and I wish I was 20 years younger. I'm 71 now and someone once said that making movies is 90 per cent hard work and 10 per cent talent, well I'll settle for 97.5 per cent hard work and 2.5 per cent talent. You do become a little weaker, as it were, as the years go by and I would like to go on making movies for another 10 or 15 years. The question is whether I can find the strength to do so but my joy in doing it and my satisfaction are undiminished.

I have stood down from most of the organisations with which I've been involved, some of them for almost 30 years. I think the charities in which I have been active need new blood. The industry bodies which I was involved with also need new blood and new ideas. They are a reflection of contemporary life and you can't reach my age and not be deeply affected by 70 years of experience. That results in a certain attitude and certain criteria by which you adjudge certain things. Your judgment is the judgment of your age. If Channel Four Television and the British Film Institute are to progress as they should, then they need new ideas, not those of an old man. Therefore it was about time I moved over and invited someone else to come

Opposite: A study in concentration

in. So I did it without any reluctance at all. I'm delighted to have had the experience and very happy that someone else should take over. In addition to that, film-making is dependent on energy and concentration and commitment. As you do get older the strength of that commitment is no less, you're just not capable of continuing at the same pace if you spread yourself too thin. Since what I want to do is to go on making movies, subjects which I just haven't been able to tackle yet, I am desperate to do it before I fall off the twig. So I think it is sensible to give up some of those extra-mural activities.

I have said already that for me filming is breathing and living and being alive. I have in some measure given up part of my private life to it as far as time at home and children and grandchildren are concerned and I don't regret that. I suppose I do regret the minutes in the hour and the hours in the day but I don't regret the decision in terms of my work. If I had not done it with the same commitment I don't think I'd still be working now. I think I would have gone under and so I don't regret it from that point of view. But I am getting older and I would like to spend more time with my grandchildren and I suppose, therefore, with a decreased workload outside of filming, they will now take a greater priority.

It was Orson Welles who once compared making movies to playing with the biggest train set in the world. He was right. I am an embarrassingly happy man.

Holding Back the Tears

As he has said, *Shadowlands* was the sort of movie which everyone had been telling Richard Attenborough he ought to have been doing for years. It's a small, intimate, tragic love story based on the story of C.S. Lewis who found love late in life with American poet Joy Gresham only to have her struck down with terminal cancer. It's a deeply moving story and one which those only conscious of Attenborough's public reputation for wearing his heart on his sleeve might have thought would quickly descend into maudlin sentimentality.

Anthony Hopkins was Attenborough's first choice to play Jack Lewis. It was their fifth film together in 20 years and Hopkins knows him better than probably any other actor. However, he insists that nothing is really pre-planned – they can go for years not seeing each other and then end up making two movies almost back to back, like *Chaplin* and *Shadowlands*. Before shooting began on *Shadowlands* Hopkins and his director had lunch to discuss elements of characterisation and other aspects of the production.

'We discussed things like how biographical the film would be,' Hopkins recalls. 'I look nothing like C.S. Lewis and I'm certainly not an intellectual giant so I was keen to play him as close to myself as possible. I also said to Dickie, using the royal "we": "We really must get rid of all the sentimentality because I hate sentimentality in a film. I can't bear watching it. Anything that is kind of dewy-eyed makes me squirm. I think if it's real it's okay but anything else I'm not comfortable with." And Dickie agreed. I think he had already made up his mind at that stage we must avoid that sort of thing. He was very strict about the scenes where Joy was dying. He shot them quite a few times. It was very hard to contain the emotion and when we cut he would try to dampen down the emotion between takes. I was very surprised when I saw the scene of me and Michael Dennison together in the finished film. It's the moment where Jack Lewis realises how much he loves Joy and how devastated he will be after her death. There were lots of tears on the first take but we did it again and again until I was sort of cried out so we could shoot the scene dry as it were. But the one he printed and used in the film was with a tear or two, which rather surprised me. But in context it was right.'

Hopkins first worked with Attenborough when he played a cameo role in Lloyd George in *Young Winston*. Since then he has appeared in *A Bridge Too Far*, *Magic*, *Chaplin* and now *Shadowlands*. In addition, there was the brief flirtation with *Gandhi* along the way. He has watched Attenborough develop as a director over the years, just as he himself has matured as an actor. Hopkins believes that cinema fashions have changed and with *Shadowlands* Attenborough is now responding to that demand.

'I think *Gandhi* was the last of his really big pictures,' he explains. 'But I think that certainly for the American market those films no longer work and I think the time has come for what is left of the film industry in this country to recognize that. I think it really came to an end with David Lean with *Ryan's Daughter* and latterly *A Passage to India* and I think Dickie was working within that framework. But fashions do change, especially in America, and I was so pleased when he offered me this. I was also rather surprised because it is a small film. He's a very emotional man and a lot of people attack him as a sentimental old fool which is just so much rubbish. Maybe there is something strange about him because he does have huge volumes of emotion which he can switch on. But he can also be quite ruthless, he knows what he wants and he gets it. He's like a workaholic bulldog, he just goes for it and he gets it.'

Both Hopkins and Attenborough knew of Debra Winger's reputation for being troublesome and tempestuous on the set. It was Hopkins who first expressed mild misgivings, although his mind was changed by the experience of actually working with her. Attenborough, however, felt that she would be the perfect Joy Gresham and after they had a clear-the-air discussion about the rumours which preceded her, persuaded Hopkins that she was perfect casting. 'I think he found out after the first meeting that it's always about the work,' says Winger, who was Oscar-nominated for her performance in *Shadowlands*. 'When I run into questions like this from a viable source, like a director I would like to work with, I explain it all. I tell them that this is what it was all about, I don't know who is right or who is wrong but this is what I fought for. It's never about the size of the dressing-room or the make-up or the camera angle, it's always about the work. The truth of the matter is that I have a pretty good relationship with all of the directors I've worked with over the past six or seven years so I guess things couldn't have got that heated.'

Hopkins remembers his first meeting with his co-star and the first thing she said to him. 'She came up and said, "I'm not difficult",' he recalls. 'I did say to Dickie that I had heard she had been difficult but then I have been difficult myself. Years ago I was an extremely difficult actor to work with. I used to attack directors because I was scared. I don't like being controlled and many directors are control freaks – Dickie isn't but a lot are. Even now I still baulk at that but now I do it more coldly. These days I just tell them if they are going to mess about then they can find another actor, I don't throw tables around any more.'

On location with Anthony Hopkins and Debra Winger for *Shadowlands*

The only difficulty which occurred during the shooting of *Shadowlands* came over a publicity picture that the studio wanted taken. Debra Winger was unhappy about it, but she was surprised to find that her co-star was standing four-square beside her. 'There was a studio decision to take pictures of us looking sexy in a pose that had nothing to do with the film,' explains Hopkins, taking up the story. 'I told them they would have to call it off because they would upset the whole apple-cart by trying to portray a film that wasn't there. I said: "You will not only have me to contend with, you will also have Miss Winger to contend with and you do not want to have the two of us on your back." So in the end they decided not to go ahead with the photograph. They were trying to manipulate us and I thought we had reached a point where enough was enough. You don't have to do everything they ask you. I like to be as amenable and friendly as possible but they were trying to push the limits too far.'

Already conditioned to expect English reserve, Debra Winger was astonished to find herself being supported in the row by Hopkins. 'It was a very interesting phenomenon.' she says. 'From the beginning of my career I got to work with people who were at the pinnacle of their success, such as John

Travolta and Richard Gere. They would roll over when they were faced by a situation like this because if you're a product of that system then you play by their rules. I thought: "Tony won't like to make waves. He thinks I'm difficult, he'll just roll too." But he didn't. I've never had anyone stand up for me like that before and I learned a great lesson from that. I realised you have to put everything in its place. You can't pick fights just because you have the energy to do it. There are a lot of people who deserve it so you have to save it for the right ones.'

By one of those strange but true coincidences Debra Winger had just finished reading *The Chronicles of Narnia* by C.S. Lewis to her seven-year-old son, Noah, the night before the *Shadowlands* script arrived. She had never seen the play or the BBC production but she had always wanted to work with Richard Attenborough. 'He had a reputation as an actors' director,' she says. 'But that doesn't really mean much unless it pans out. I would say, and this is the most important thing about him, that more than any other director I have worked with he has the most amazing respect for the actor's job. Because of that respect everything else falls into place. It serves as an inspiration to an actor, it gives you time, it strengthens your resolve because with all that respect comes an expectation of greatness on your part.

'He doesn't do line readings but he understands the text and he understands the different ways in which actors work. God knows in this film Tony and I couldn't have been any more different, we were like night and day, and that means a director has to be very astute. He can't use a different style for the two actors but in the end I think you both move towards his style. I don't think it's very helpful for a director to cater to an individual actor. Hopefully you will all speak a language which is understandable to the others and after a few weeks you get a sort of shorthand.'

Attenborough has admitted that he sees something of his own mother in the character of Joy Gresham. During filming Debra Winger recalls him telling her stories of his own childhood and his mother. Winger says she felt that he was trying to make the point to her that a mother could be strong but that didn't mean to say she had to rule the roost.

'I think he was trying to tell me that it was a collaborative thing,' she continues. 'Obviously he got a lot of that at home because he is wildly secure in himself and at the same time able to let others in, which is very rare. I think Richard has an amazing respect for family, which I found very touching both for myself and Noah, I think that comes across clearly in the films that he makes.'

Shadowlands revolves around three emotional high-points. The first is the scene in the chapel when Lewis realises his strength of feeling, the second is Joy's death scene, and the third is the most powerful scene of all. After she is dead Lewis and her young son Douglas, played by Joey Mazzello, are in the attic of their home. Together they come to terms with the magnitude of their loss in a deeply emotional scene which has even the hardest of audiences in floods of tears. But for that scene to work then the rest of the film has to be carefully gauged and paced. Once again Attenborough and Lesley Walker had work to do in the cutting-room. 'Because of his experience with *Chaplin* he was keen to get the film as close to two hours and ten minutes as possible,' she remembers. 'At one point he wanted to get it to two hours exactly but that would have simply destroyed it. We got it down and then we put stuff back and in the end we got it to two hours 12 minutes.

'The hardest thing in *Shadowlands* was in holding back the emotion and that's what made it one of the most difficult films I've had to cut. The idea was to let the audience laugh or cry. But only when you wanted them to and not any other time. I hope we achieved that because in that scene in the attic when they are finally allowed to cry they usually do let themselves go. It's like riding a horse, you rein it in a bit and then let it go, it's just a question of getting the balance. I think you have to use your own emotions to judge the pace of the scenes and Richard is wonderful at that. Everyone goes on about how he cries. It's true but that's what, certainly in this film, the audience was supposed to do. My first assembly of the film was about two hours 50 minutes and it had no music in it except for a piece which I had begged George Fenton to write for me for my own guidance. I remembered what had happened with *Cry Freedom* so this time there was only Richard, Diana, me and my assistants. He was a total mess at the end of the film, we all were. I still cry at it. Even though it was longer in that version it still had that balance. It's a trick, you just know it instinctively.'

The music for *Shadowlands*, as in every Attenborough film, was desperately important. Attenborough knew exactly what he wanted for this film and he also knew to whom he should turn to get it. Over the years George Fenton has become Attenborough's favourite composer. He wrote the music for *Gandhi* and *Cry Freedom* and would have worked on other movies but for conflicting schedules. The director knew he was perfect for the job when he came to direct *Shadowlands*.

There are parallels in his championing of Fenton with his championing of his actors. Fenton was known mainly for his television and stage work when Attenborough gave him his major movie break with *Gandhi*. Once again, as in the case of Ben Kingsley, it was the director's son Michael who brought them together. Fenton finds Attenborough an inspirational presence. He admits that in the three films they have done together he has grown as a composer and that is, in large measure, due to the encouragement and trust which comes from the director.

'Usually when a composer is hired to write the music for the film he is involved as almost the last part of the process,' Fenton explains. 'But that has never been the case with Dickie. I've never worked with him without going along on location. Even when he was previewing *Cry Freedom* in the States he took Lesley Walker and me along with him. He is very musical himself and he has a great sense of what he wants for a scene. He is also very good at instinctively knowing which are the best or most appropriate bits of the music. That level of interest and appreciation is very helpful for a composer.'

Fenton's first job for Richard Attenborough was scoring *Gandhi*, and in that experience he came across a facet of Attenborough which took him by surprise. 'The opening titles of a film are very important for a composer,' Fenton explains. 'The audience is conditioned to expect music and you can then introduce it at any other time in the picture once you've got over the hurdle of that first cue. For *Gandhi*, of course, there are no opening credits, the film starts with bird song and various sound effects and I was having enormous problems in getting the first piece of music right. Dickie kept asking and eventually I told him that I couldn't come up with anything which I thought would do him justice. I was at my wits' end. He had spent the best part of 20 years trying to get this film off the ground and here I was as almost the final piece of the jigsaw and I felt terrible because I thought I was letting him down. But when I told him about the problem he said, "It's only a movie, darling. It's not about life or death, or family, or relationships. It's only a movie."'

Happily, and thanks in large part to Attenborough's equanimity, Fenton was able to come up with that vital first cue and all of the others in what turned out to be an Oscar-nominated score for *Gandhi*. But later in the process of recording the soundtrack there was another landmark incident in the relationship between the composer and his director.

'I had been out to India a couple of times and I had had the wonderful experience of working with Ravi Shankar,' Fenton recalls. 'I had then come back and written the music which was going to be played by the Indian musicians. I knew I had written it as well as I could but I wasn't quite sure if it was what we wanted in the sense of whether it would actually work when it was played by the musicians. The great fear that any composer has is of having his music dropped from the film. When I mentioned my misgivings to Dickie he just said, "Well if it doesn't work you'll just have to go back and start again." I realised then that the thought of not using the music had simply not occurred to him. He had hired me to do a job and he believed that I could do the job, otherwise he wouldn't have taken me on in the first place.'

As Lesley Walker suggests, the music for *Shadowlands* was absolutely vital in maintaining the balance between sentiment and sentimentality which the movie had to strike if it was to work. Fenton had been on location before to soak up atmosphere but in *Shadowlands* he was at Magdalen College, primarily because the choristers were working to music he had already written. The opening anthem for *Shadowlands* sounds like an original piece of authentic English Tudor music. In fact it was written specifically for the movie by George Fenton.

'I must have listened to about 100 hours of Tudor music,' says Fenton. 'But Dickie never really liked any of the pieces I put up. There was always something not right. We were at his house and I started to play a piece on the piano as an example of what I thought the opening should sound like and Dickie just seized on it. He told me that was exactly what we needed and I went away and worked on that and it eventually became the opening anthem.'

With or without the music the big emotional scenes in *Shadowlands* were tough on the actors but both Anthony Hopkins and Debra Winger were aware of how much care Attenborough was taking to make sure they could give of their best when it was required of them. For Hopkins the key thing is to relax

Old friends. Anthony Hopkins and Richard Attenborough on *Shadowlands*, their fifth film together

because if he is relaxed then he knows that invariably he can do it. However, he admits to feeling slightly nauseous with apprehension on the morning when he was to film the attic scene with Joey Mazzello.

'Joey is a very good actor and it was actually his vulnerability in this scene that tipped me over the edge emotionally,' he recalls. 'We did the scene about four times and Dickie made sure that everything was kept very quiet, very relaxed, and very conducive to working. He keeps noise to a minimum, they call you to the set when they actually need you, and you do it without any fanfare. Sometimes it may go wrong but you take your chances.'

Debra Winger was more concerned for Joey Mazzello than she was for her own performance when the time came to shoot these scenes. She had her son Noah with her during filming. Noah is only a few years younger than Joey but she admits that her young co-star was more in control than anyone during those scenes. 'You always have to take your cue from the children,' she explains. 'With Joey I felt very protective because of Noah and I tried to talk to him about acting technique and everything and he said: "Oh, I just think of something sad." He wouldn't even tell me what he thought of! I've known other child actors who bite the insides of their mouths till they bleed to make themselves cry. But Joey was off on his own deal and Tony and I were just struggling to tread water. I think he was more in control than either of us. He was concerned that we were working too hard. I had long chats with Joey because I worry about child actors working too much. My son was on the set too and I had to keep making sure that he was alright as the story progressed. My character dies and even though it is only acting it's like visiting a place and a possibility. I think what scares children is not something happening, children are very strong in the face of things, but they get scared when they have to think of things that could happen. So I watched out for Joey but I didn't change anything for him.'

'We laughed a great deal together during the death scenes,' says Hopkins. 'That was very therapeutic and Joey was in on that. Dickie is a very emotional man which everybody knows but it is a genuine emotion and we shouldn't knock him for that. He made us laugh all the time between takes, which was marvellous because otherwise it would simply have got darker and darker.'

Attenborough's actors, especially the Americans, who are perhaps less used to being taken seriously, would walk over hot coals for him. Yet he has remained for a long time almost a caricature within some sectors of the British film industry. Younger directors have tended not to take him seriously. Regardless of the fact that many of them are only working because he chose, unlike a lot of them, to stay here and maintain some kind of British film industry, he is considered by some as something of an old fogey, a 'Spitting Image' puppet made flesh. Anthony Hopkins tells the story of a visit to the set of *Shadowlands* by Alan Parker, foremost among the angry young men of the British cinema in the Seventies.

'He was casting this film I've just done with him called *The Road to Welville* and he wanted me to play the lead so he came down for a chat,' says Hopkins. 'He knew Dickie, of course, and he said to me, "It's very relaxed here, I wish my sets were like this." Then he went on, "You know," he said, "we always used to laugh at Dickie because he was always so nice. But he is nice isn't he." So I worked with Alan Parker and he was right, his set is a little more serious, a little more tense, and he doesn't laugh much. But he's a wonderful director as well.'

Along with perhaps Wendy Woods in *Cry Freedom*, Joy Gresham is one of the few substantial women's roles in Attenborough movies. She is certainly the only one who gets equal screen time with her male counterpart. Attenborough has in the past been criticised, especially in *Chaplin*, for being misogynistic in his directorial outlook. He himself has denied this and Debra Winger is adamant that she didn't find anything to bear out those criticisms. 'Even though a lot of people on *Shadowlands* had worked together before I never felt as though I was coming into a boys' club or anything like that,' she insists. 'Yes the story was always primarily about C.S. Lewis but that was the writer William Nicholson, not Richard Attenborough. I came in and did what I could, probably just enough to make Joy discoverable, but I always felt that what I was doing was essential. Dickie will print the takes that he likes and he'll print things that make you feel essential because then you'll do your best work.

'I think Richard Attenborough is a master of what he does and I don't use that term lightly. I think he is a master film-maker and anyone who can even consider arguing that point doesn't even have the sense he was born with. I had heard in the past that people have trouble with his movies because he is sentimental but I think *Shadowlands* disproves that. You have the most sentimental subject possible for a director and he veered as far away from sentiment as he could. But what is a darkened movie theatre for if not to be touched at some length or drawn to anger or tears. It's there to explore the emotions and to have an experience and Richard Attenborough fulfils that.'

Afterword: The Barber Said, 'Thank God!'

William Goldman memorably described Richard Attenborough as 'the nicest, most decent human being I have met in the motion picture business.' The public perception of Hollywood is one of a town where nice guys finish last. Yet for 25 years they have been taking meetings with Richard Attenborough and assiduously returning his calls. Instrumental in that is his agent, Marti Baum.

Marti Baum is more than Richard Attenborough's agent, he is a loyal and trusted friend. The two men are of an age and their relationship goes back over 30 years. Baum's credentials in Hollywood are impeccable. When a group of young agents left the mighty William Morris Agency to set up on their own they needed a 'father figure' for guidance. The man they turned to was Marti Baum, and under his tutelage and supervision these renegades became the now all-powerful Creative Artists Agency headed by super-agent Mike Ovitz. From their ultra-modern offices on Wilshire Boulevard in Los Angeles, CAA are Hollywood's ultimate power brokers.

Baum recognises the truth of what William Goldman says but also maintains it would be a gross simplification for anyone to assume that there is no room in the movie business for people like Attenborough. It needn't be an industry where nice guys finish last. 'We have bad people who have survived and we have nice people who have survived,' he says. 'You can't generalise. The simple fact is that Richard Attenborough is respected for his integrity and the subjects that he chooses, which in all cases have something to say about the condition of mankind and how it can be improved. Sometimes that is commercially acceptable and sometimes it isn't. He's really deeply entrenched in doing films that have human relationships that are honest and sincere. Hopefully the audience will first be enriched by the morality of what the people on the screen are doing and also entertained. But the primary function is to be

Richard Attenborough and agent Marti Baum on the morning after the Oscar night before

entertained – you cannot be a minister of the gospel in moving pictures. If you can subtly get a message in on the side then that's gravy.'

Baum and Attenborough have stood shoulder to shoulder on Wilshire Boulevard and fought their battles against the Hollywood establishment and more often than not emerged on the side of the angels. They have scored some spectacular coups in their time but none as big as their achievements with *Gandhi*.

The multi-Oscar winner was made without a penny of Hollywood money. The funding, entirely and brilliantly gathered by Jake Eberts, had come from diverse sources, including pension funds for Britain's miners and postmen which both did rather well out of the finished product. But it was Marti Baum who turned it from a movie into a sensation. Having finished the movie, Attenborough needed a distribution deal from one of the American majors to guarantee the film's box-office success. Marti Baum undertook to get the head of each studio into a viewing theatre to see the movie in the space of little more than 48 hours. The result was a feeding frenzy which went a long way to ensuring that Attenborough's prize project got the treatment he had always known it deserved. And for Marti Baum it was no less than he believed his client was entitled to.

'*Gandhi* involved years of hard labour for us in Hollywood,' recalls the man dubbed 'Agent Orange' by veteran Broadway producer Cy Feuer because of his once flame-red hair. 'Joe Levine said he was going to do it then he wouldn't do it. All the studios said they were going to do it then they didn't do it. Up until the very last second when we by then had the help of Jake Eberts and Goldcrest we couldn't get that picture going. It was very painful. At one point one studio told us: "Yes, you've got a deal, we're in." Dickie and I were celebrating the fact that they had said yes when they called two hours later to say they had changed their mind. In each case I could only tell him: "Never give up. Don't quit."'

Neither Attenborough nor Baum was prepared to quit on *Gandhi* and in the end their faith was rewarded. Their next picture together was another testing one but for different reasons. Funding for *A Chorus Line* was not a problem but the critical savaging it received could have ruined less resilient directors. It was Marti Baum who advised Attenborough to take the movie and he remains unrepentant.

'I can't tell you anything other than that if the same circumstances existed today I would still advise him to do it,' he says with candour. 'It was a beautifully constructed piece. It was faithful to the best parts of the show and he opened it up into a further level of depth in terms of the characters and their relationships than the show ever did. He explored more deeply the stories which they were telling only by anecdote on the stage. He did a terrific job and there were some critics who liked the movie very much. But it was a failure, there's no question about it and there were a lot of critics who were very savage. This was a good picture and its failure still hurts but I don't regret advising him to do it and I don't regret the work he did on it. I'm very proud of it and I would show it to anyone as an example of the fact that beside doing movies of social significance he can also do something as straightforwardly entertaining as a musical. The choreography and the camerawork were terrific. This happens occasionally. Some films get killed for no good reason, it just happens.'

Filming *Chaplin* was another torrid experience for Baum and Attenborough as they did battle for Robert Downey at Universal and then for the movie itself at Carolco. Attenborough has always felt that the story of putting this film together is worth a book in itself. He even toyed with the idea of writing one with the cryptic title *The Barber said 'Thank God!'*. 'We had a very hectic time getting *Chaplin* set up,' says Baum with commendable restraint. 'It was originally supposed to go at Universal and then it was put into turnaround after $8 million had been spent on pre-production. They were almost ready to start shooting when they stopped production. Then I had to shop the picture round and find another home for it, which I finally did. During the process of shopping it around I used to get a haircut and manicure every Friday at the old Beverly Hills Hotel where the barber is English. His name is Tony. They tore the hotel down for refurbishing and he is now the chief barber at the Beverly Hilton. He would listen to me because I would always have to take telephone calls while I was in his chair about what was happening. Since he was English and Chaplin was English and Dickie is English he was taking a keen interest in whether we were going to get it set up. Finally, on the day that we got the word that we had found a home and

Chaplin was going to be done, I got the news on the telephone and he had his clippers in the air. And I said, "Okay we have Chaplin closed."

'He raised his hands and shouted, "Thank God."

'So when I called Dickie to tell him that I had closed the deal he said: "That's wonderful. Who knows?" I said the barber knows and he said, "What did he say."

'I told him, "The barber said Thank God."'

After the commercial failures of *Cry Freedom* and *Chaplin*, especially in America, both Attenborough and Baum knew that they needed either a solid commercial success or at the very least a critical hit. With *Shadowlands* in large measure they have delivered both. 'First of all the reviews were universally the best reviews Dickie has had since *Gandhi*,' says Baum with some pride. 'So his stature has gone up since *Shadowlands*. The picture speaks for itself, it is beautifully directed and beautifully acted. Also *The Remains of the Day*, which got all those nominations, took less money than *Shadowlands* even though it had been out about ten weeks longer. It would have been nice to have had a break-out blockbuster but, second to that, this was definitely a mark up not a mark back.'

Next to *Gandhi*, Attenborough's other long-cherished project is a film biography of Thomas Paine, the revolutionary and author of the renowned book *The Rights of Man*. It is a subject and a project close to the director's heart. Baum will be the man who will have to set up the meetings and judge when the omens are right to make the pitch for *Tom Paine*. But he acknowledges that it will not be easy. 'Right now the story comes out at about four hours and that's a problem in itself,' he says. 'You can't do two two-hour movies any more. The fact is that Tom Paine, aside from playing a significant part in the American revolution, played a significant part in the French revolution and that's two movies to begin with. The problems at the moment are difficult and my opinion is that when Dickie has a smash hit at the box office he can do anything. *Tom Paine* isn't going to go away and we have to strike at the most propitious moment to make that picture because of the size of it and the story it attempts to tell. We've had offers to do it on television but we can't hit the marketplace right now so we have to wait until Dickie's star has risen a little higher.'

In the meantime Marti Baum can thrive on the challenge of having a hot new actor to represent. After his success as John Hammond in *Jurassic Park* Attenborough is once again back in front of the camera in a role which could have been tailor-made for him. 'He is playing Santa Claus in *Miracle on 34th Street* for John Hughes who made the *Home Alone* pictures and directed by an exciting new young director called Les Mayfield,' explains Baum. 'Acting is something he spent many years doing and having fun with and now he's doing it again. I'm touting him as an exciting newcomer, especially when you consider how successful his last picture as an actor was. He tells me privately that the real reason he is doing this picture is to show his grandchildren that he has some standing in the community.'

His return to acting is only temporary, however. Attenborough insists that he could not foresee a situation where he would go back if it meant giving up directing. Making movies is what he wants to do more than anything else and that means that he and Baum will once again be trying to film their impossible dreams. It's a challenge which Attenborough thrives on. Baum probably does too, he's just a little more reluctant to show it. 'Both of us would love nothing more than an easy situation where the money is there, the budget is set, the picture is approved, the stars are in and we make the movie,' he says. 'It wouldn't be the same but I guess the fulfilment of the effort in success – in the sense that the movie is made – gets more appreciation for the work that went behind it. But before that golden moment comes, when the movie deal is put together and the movie is going to get made, the doubt and the intransigence of the people that you are talking to and the disappointments are heart-breaking. The thing that keeps Dickie and I and Diana going is that we have an infinite belief in each other and we have an ever-present sense of optimism.

'If I thought of the odds when I got up in the morning to make one of these things happen I'd stay in bed all day. I wouldn't get out of bed because the odds would be at least 100-1 against me. But I don't think of the odds, I think of it optimistically and that's the only way to do it.'

And that's Dickie Attenborough, a man for whom filming is living . . . and living optimistically.

Appendix

Richard Attenborough: A Filmography

I DIRECTOR

Oh! What a Lovely War (1969)
144 mins

> Director: Richard Attenborough
> Script: Len Deighton
> Producers: Brian Duffy and Richard Attenborough
> Associate producer: Mack Davidson
> Photography: Gerry Turpin
> Production design: Don Ashton
> Editor: Kevin Connor
> Music: Alfred Ralston
> Choreography: Eleanor Fazan

CAST: Dirk Bogarde, Phyllis Calvert, Jean-Pierre Cassel, John Clements, John Gielgud, Jack Hawkins, John Mills, Kenneth More, Laurence Olivier, Michael Redgrave, Ralph Richardson, Maggie Smith, Susannah York.

Young Winston (1972)
157 mins

> Director: Richard Attenborough
> Script: Carl Foreman
> Producer: Carl Foreman
> Associate producer: Harold Buck
> Photography: Gerry Turpin
> Production design: Don Ashton, Geoffrey Drake
> Editor: Kevin Connor

Music: Alfred Ralston

CAST: Simon Ward, Robert Shaw, Anne Bancroft, John Mills, Jack Hawkins, Ian Holm, Anthony Hopkins, Patrick Magee, Edward Woodward.

A Bridge Too Far (1977)
175 mins

Director: Richard Attenborough
Script: William Goldman
Producers: Joseph E. Levine and Richard Levine
Associate producer: Michael Stanley-Evans
Photography: Geoffrey Unsworth
Production designer: Terence Marsh
Art direction: Stuart Craig, Alan Tomkins, Roy Stannard
Editor: Anthony Gibbs
Production manager: Terence Clegg
Music: John Addison
First assistant director: David Tomblin

CAST: Dirk Bogarde, James Caan, Michael Caine, Sean Connery, Edward Fox, Elliott Gould, Gene Hackman, Anthony Hopkins, Hardy Kruger, Laurence Olivier, Ryan O'Neal, Robert Redford, Maximilian Schell, Liv Ullman.

Magic (1978)
107 mins

Director: Richard Attenborough
Script: William Goldman
Producers: Joseph E. Levine and Richard Levine
Photography: Victor Kemper
Production design: Terence Marsh
Editor: John Bloom
Music: Jerry Goldsmith

CAST: Anthony Hopkins, Ann-Margret, Burgess Meredith, Ed Lauter.

Gandhi (1982)
188 mins

Director: Richard Attenborough
Script: John Briley
Producer: Richard Attenborough
Executive producer: Michael Stanley-Evans
Photography: Billy Williams, Ronnie Taylor
Production design: Stuart Craig
Editor: John Bloom
In charge of production: Terence Clegg
Music: Ravi Shankar and George Fenton
First assistant director: David Tomblin

CAST: Ben Kingsley, Candice Bergen, Edward Fox, John Gielgud, Trevor Howard, John Mills, Martin Sheen, Rohini Hattangady, Athol Fugard, Gunter Maria Halmer, Saeed Jaffrey, Geraldine James, Alyque Padamsee, Amrish Puri, Roshan Seth.

A Chorus Line (1985)
118 mins

Director: Richard Attenborough
Script: Arnold Schulman
Producers: Cy Feuer and Ernest H. Martin
Photography: Ronnie Taylor
Production design: Patrizia von Brandenstein
Editor: John Bloom
Music and lyrics: Marvin Hamlisch, Edward Kleban
Choreography: Jeffrey Hornaday

CAST: Michael Douglas, Alyson Reed, Terrence Mann, Michael Blevins, Yamil Borges, Jan Gan Boyd, Gregg Burge, Cameron English, Tony Fields, Nicole Fosse, Vikki Frederick, Janet Jones, Michelle Johnston, Audrey Landers, Pam Klinger, Charles McGowan, Justin Ross, Blane Savage, Matt West.

Cry Freedom (1987)
159 mins

Director: Richard Attenborough
Script: John Briley
Producer: Richard Attenborough

Co-producers: Norman Spencer and John Briley
In charge of production: Terence Clegg
Photography: Ronnie Taylor
Production design: Stuart Craig
Editor: Lesley Walker
Music: George Fenton and Jonas Gwangwa
First assistant director: David Tomblin

CAST: Kevin Kline, Penelope Wilton, Denzel Washington, John Hargreaves, Alec McCowen, Kevin McNally, Zakes Mokae, John Thaw.

Chaplin (1992)
144 mins

Director: Richard Attenborough
Script: William Boyd and Bryan Forbes and William Goldman
Story: Diana Hawkins
Producers: Richard Attenborough and Mario Kassar
Co-producer: Terence Clegg
Associate producer: Diana Hawkins
Photography: Sven Nykvist
Production design: Stuart Craig
Editor: Anne V. Coates
Music: John Barry
First assistant director: David Tomblin

CAST: Robert Downey Jnr, Dan Aykroyd, Geraldine Chaplin, Kevin Dunn, Anthony Hopkins, Milla Jovovich, Moira Kelly, Kevin Kline, Diane Lane, Penelope Ann Miller, Paul Rhys, John Thaw, Marisa Tomei, Nancy Travis, James Woods.

Shadowlands (1993)
131 mins

Director: Richard Attenborough
Script: William Nicholson
Producers: Richard Attenborough, Brian Eastman
Executive producer: Terence Clegg
Co-producer: Diana Hawkins
Photography: Roger Pratt
Production design: Stuart Craig
Editor: Lesley Walker
Music: George Fenton

CAST: Anthony Hopkins, Debra Winger, Edward Hardwicke, John Wood, Michael Denison, Joseph Mazzello.

II PRODUCER

The Angry Silence, 1960 (co-produced with Bryan Forbes)
Whistle Down the Wind, 1961
The L-shaped Room, 1962 (co-produced with Bryan Forbes)
Séance on a Wet Afternoon, 1964
Oh! What A Lovely War, 1969 (co-produced with Brian Duffy)
Gandhi, 1982
Cry Freedom, 1987
Chaplin, 1992 (co-produced with Mario Kassar)
Shadowlands, 1993 (co-produced with Brian Eastman)

III ACTOR

In Which We Serve, 1942
Schweik's New Adventures, 1943
The Hundred Pound Window, 1944
Journey Together, 1945
A Matter of Life and Death, 1946
School for Secrets, 1947
The Man Within, 1947
Dancing with Crime, 1947
Brighton Rock, 1947
London Belongs to Me, 1948
The Guinea Pig, 1948
The Lost People, 1948
Boys in Brown, 1949
Morning Departure, 1949
Hell is Sold Out, 1950
The Magic Box, 1950
Gift Horse, 1951
Father's Doing Fine, 1952
Eight O'Clock Walk, 1953
The Ship that Died of Shame, 1954
Private's Progress, 1955
The Baby and the Battleship, 1955
Brothers in Law, 1956
The Scamp, 1957

Dunkirk, 1957
The Man Upstairs, 1958
Sea of Sand, 1958
Danger Within, 1958
I'm All Right Jack, 1959
Jetstorm, 1959
SOS Pacific, 1959
The Angry Silence, 1960
The League of Gentlemen, 1960
Only Two Can Play, 1961
All Night Long, 1961
The Dock Brief, 1962
The Great Escape, 1962
The Third Secret, 1963
Séance on a Wet Afternoon, 1964
Guns at Batasi, 1964
Flight of the Phoenix, 1965
The Sand Pebbles, 1966
Dr Dolittle, 1966
The Bliss of Mrs Blossom, 1967
Only When I Larf, 1967
The Magic Christian, 1967
The Last Grenade, 1969
A Severed Head, 1969
David Copperfield, 1969
Loot, 1969
10 Rillington Place, 1970
And Then There Were None, 1974
Rosebud, 1974
Brannigan, 1974
Conduct Unbecoming, 1974
The Chess Players, 1977
The Human Factor, 1979
Jurassic Park, 1993
Miracle on 34th Street, 1994

Index